STAND FIRM
Putting on the Full Armor of God

AUBREY COLEMAN

Study Suggestions

We believe that the Bible is true, trustworthy, and timeless and that it is vitally important for all believers. These study suggestions are intended to help you more effectively study Scripture as you seek to know and love God through His Word.

SUGGESTED STUDY TOOLS

- A Bible

- A double-spaced, printed copy of the Scripture passages that this study covers. You can use a website like *www.biblegateway.com* to copy the text of a passage and print out a double-spaced copy to be able to mark on easily

- A journal to write notes or prayers

- Pens, colored pencils, and highlighters

- A dictionary to look up unfamiliar words

HOW TO USE THIS STUDY

Begin your study time in prayer. Ask God to reveal Himself to you, to help you understand what you are reading, and to transform you with His Word (Psalm 119:18).

Before you read what is written in each day of the study itself, read the assigned passages of Scripture for that day. Use your double-spaced copy to circle, underline, highlight, draw arrows, and mark in any way you would like to help you dig deeper as you work through a passage.

Read the daily written content provided for the current study day.

Answer the questions that appear at the end of each study day.

HOW TO STUDY THE BIBLE

The inductive method provides tools for deeper and more intentional Bible study. To study the Bible inductively, work through the steps below after reading background information on the book.

1 OBSERVATION & COMPREHENSION
Key question: What does the text say?

After reading the daily Scripture in its entirety at least once, begin working with smaller portions of the Scripture. Read a passage of Scripture repetitively, and then mark the following items in the text:

- Key or repeated words and ideas
- Key themes
- Transition words (Ex: therefore, but, because, if/then, likewise, etc.)
- Lists
- Comparisons and contrasts
- Commands
- Unfamiliar words (look these up in a dictionary)
- Questions you have about the text

2 INTERPRETATION
Key question: What does the text mean?

Once you have annotated the text, work through the following steps to help you interpret its meaning:

- Read the passage in other versions for a better understanding of the text.
- Read cross-references to help interpret Scripture with Scripture.
- Paraphrase or summarize the passage to check for understanding.
- Identify how the text reflects the metanarrative of Scripture, which is the story of creation, fall, redemption, and restoration.
- Read trustworthy commentaries if you need further insight into the meaning of the passage.

3 APPLICATION
Key Question: How should the truth of this passage change me?

Bible study is not merely an intellectual pursuit. The truths about God, ourselves, and the gospel that we discover in Scripture should produce transformation in our hearts and lives. Answer the following questions as you consider what you have learned in your study:

- What attributes of God's character are revealed in the passage?

    Consider places where the text directly states the character of God, as well as how His character is revealed through His words and actions.

- What do I learn about myself in light of who God is?

    Consider how you fall short of God's character, how the text reveals your sin nature, and what it says about your new identity in Christ.

- How should this truth change me?

    A passage of Scripture may contain direct commands telling us what to do or warnings about sins to avoid in order to help us grow in holiness. Other times our application flows out of seeing ourselves in light of God's character. As we pray and reflect on how God is calling us to change in light of His Word, we should be asking questions like, "How should I pray for God to change my heart?" and "What practical steps can I take toward cultivating habits of holiness?"

THE ATTRIBUTES OF GOD

ETERNAL
God has no beginning and no end. He always was, always is, and always will be.

HAB. 1:12 / REV. 1:8 / IS. 41:4

FAITHFUL
God is incapable of anything but fidelity. He is loyally devoted to His plan and purpose.

2 TIM. 2:13 / DEUT. 7:9
HEB. 10:23

GOOD
God is pure; there is no defilement in Him. He is unable to sin, and all He does is good.

GEN. 1:31 / PS. 34:8 / PS. 107:1

GRACIOUS
God is kind, giving us gifts and benefits we do not deserve.

2 KINGS 13:23 / PS. 145:8
IS. 30:18

HOLY
God is undefiled and unable to be in the presence of defilement. He is sacred and set-apart.

REV. 4:8 / LEV. 19:2 / HAB. 1:13

INCOMPREHENSIBLE & TRANSCENDENT
God is high above and beyond human understanding. He is unable to be fully known.

PS. 145:3 / IS. 55:8-9
ROM. 11:33-36

IMMUTABLE
God does not change. He is the same yesterday, today, and tomorrow.

1 SAM. 15:29 / ROM. 11:29
JAMES 1:17

INFINITE
God is limitless. He exhibits all of His attributes perfectly and boundlessly.

ROM. 11:33-36 / IS. 40:28
PS. 147:5

JEALOUS
God is desirous of receiving the praise and affection He rightly deserves.

EX. 20:5 / DEUT. 4:23-24
JOSH. 24:19

JUST
God governs in perfect justice. He acts in accordance with justice. In Him, there is no wrongdoing or dishonesty.

IS. 61:8 / DEUT. 32:4 / PS. 146:7-9

LOVING
God is eternally, enduringly, steadfastly loving and affectionate. He does not forsake or betray His covenant love.

JN. 3:16 / EPH. 2:4-5 / 1 JN. 4:16

MERCIFUL
God is compassionate, withholding from us the wrath that we deserve.

TITUS 3:5 / PS. 25:10
LAM. 3:22-23

OMNIPOTENT
God is all-powerful; His strength is unlimited.

MAT. 19:26 / JOB 42:1-2
JER. 32:27

OMNIPRESENT
God is everywhere; His presence is near and permeating.

PROV. 15:3 / PS. 139:7-10
JER. 23:23-24

OMNISCIENT
God is all-knowing; there is nothing unknown to Him.

PS. 147:4 / I JN. 3:20
HEB. 4:13

PATIENT
God is long-suffering and enduring. He gives ample opportunity for people to turn toward Him.

ROM. 2:4 / 2 PET. 3:9 / PS. 86:15

SELF-EXISTENT
God was not created but exists by His power alone.

PS. 90:1-2 / JN. 1:4 / JN. 5:26

SELF-SUFFICIENT
God has no needs and depends on nothing, but everything depends on God.

IS. 40:28-31 / ACTS 17:24-25
PHIL. 4:19

SOVEREIGN
God governs over all things; He is in complete control.

COL. 1:17 / PS. 24:1-2
1 CHRON. 29:11-12

TRUTHFUL
God is our measurement of what is fact. By Him we are able to discern true and false.

JN. 3:33 / ROM. 1:25 / JN. 14:6

WISE
God is infinitely knowledgeable and is judicious with His knowledge.

IS. 46:9-10 / IS. 55:9 / PROV. 3:19

WRATHFUL
God stands in opposition to all that is evil. He enacts judgment according to His holiness, righteousness, and justice.

PS. 69:24 / JN. 3:36 / ROM. 1:18

METANARRATIVE OF SCRIPTURE

Creation

In the beginning, God created the universe. He made the world and everything in it. He created humans in His own image to be His representatives on the earth.

Fall

The first humans, Adam and Eve, disobeyed God by eating from the fruit of the Tree of Knowledge of Good and Evil. Their disobedience impacted the whole world. The punishment for sin is death, and because of Adam's original sin, all humans are sinful and condemned to death.

Redemption

God sent His Son to become a human and redeem His people. Jesus Christ lived a sinless life but died on the cross to pay the penalty for sin. He resurrected from the dead and ascended into heaven. All who put their faith in Jesus are saved from death and freely receive the gift of eternal life.

Restoration

One day, Jesus Christ will return again and restore all that sin destroyed. He will usher in a new heaven and new earth where all who trust in Him will live eternally with glorified bodies in the presence of God.

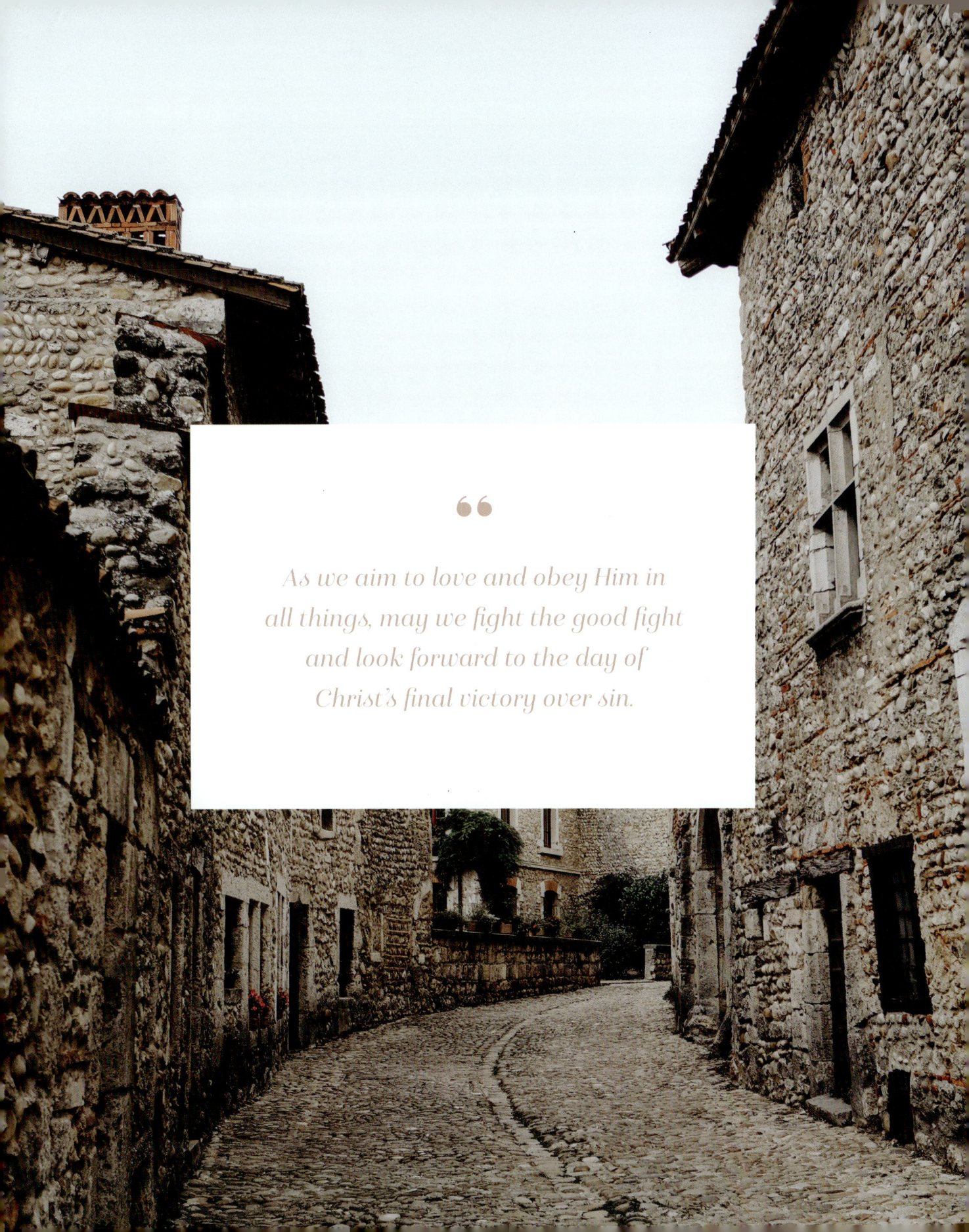

> As we aim to love and obey Him in all things, may we fight the good fight and look forward to the day of Christ's final victory over sin.

in this study

week 1

The Battle Before Us 15
Strength in the Lord 19
Know Your Enemy 23
The Full Armor of God 27
The Belt of Truth 31
Scripture Memory 35
Weekly Reflection 36

week 2

Breastplate of Righteousness 39
Sandaled with Readiness for the Gospel of Peace 43
Shield of Faith 47
Helmet of Salvation 51
Sword of the Spirit 55
Scripture Memory 59
Weekly Reflection 60

week 3

Devoted to Prayer   63
Perseverance   67
Intercede for the Saints   71
The Gospel Goes Forth   75
Victory in Jesus   79
Scripture Memory   83
Weekly Reflection   84

extra resources

Ephesians 6:10-18   12
The Full Armor of God   86
Old Testament References   88
What is the Gospel?   90

Ephesians 6:10-18

Finally, be strengthened by the Lord and by his vast strength. Put on the full armor of God so that you can stand against the schemes of the devil. For our struggle is not against flesh and blood, but against the rulers, against the authorities, against the cosmic powers of this darkness, against evil, spiritual forces in the heavens. For this reason take up the full armor of God, so that you may be able to resist in the evil day, and having prepared everything, to take your stand. Stand, therefore, with truth like a belt around your waist, righteousness like armor on your chest, and your feet sandaled with readiness for the gospel of peace. In every situation take up the shield of faith with which you can extinguish all the flaming arrows of the evil one. Take the helmet of salvation and the sword of the Spirit—which is the word of God. Pray at all times in the Spirit with every prayer and request, and stay alert with all perseverance and intercession for all the saints.

Read through Ephesians 6:10-18

1
Underline every noun that represents what God has already provided for us through Jesus Christ.

2
Circle every verb that indicates what we are to do with what God has provided us.

3
Make a list:

What God has provided for us	What we are to do with what God has provided for us

WEEK 1 / DAY 1

We must arise each day with thoughtfulness and discernment of the Lord's instruction.

INTRODUCTION

The Battle Before Us

READ EPHESIANS 6:10-20

It is difficult for most of us to imagine someone going into war unprotected. Few would step into the heat of battle without some kind of protection, for without that protection, great harm would likely come in the form of a wound or even death. We ask, *who would take that risk?* Yet, the truth is, there are many, unprotected and unaware, who brave battles each day—not in the sense of physical war but the spiritual war that rages around us. That is why the Apostle Paul uses this language of war to instruct the church of Ephesus (Ephesians 6:10-20).

Recipients of the letter of Ephesians would have lived during the time of the Roman Empire, but Paul draws inspiration from a time well before the era this letter was written. What is often overlooked when studying the armor of God is the references to God's armor in the book of Isaiah and other books of the Old Testament. Readers might assume that Paul's inspiration for the armor of God came from the wardrobe of Roman soldiers at that time. However, it was drawn from Old Testament references of God exhibiting the armor Himself. That said, Paul does employ the imagery of a Roman soldier when referencing Isaiah, imagery that his audience would easily recognize. Throughout the study, we will make a connection to the Old Testament inspiration of God's armor, while also using the example of the Roman soldier. It is important that we understand this background information because it will shape our understanding as we study the usage of the armor of God in Ephesians 6 and its intended purposes in the battle set before us.

The battle we fight is not a physical one, but a spiritual one—one fought against the evil that menaces the very world in which we live. As Christians, we are called, as representatives of God, to put on the armor He has given us so as to wage war against the evil that threatens to undo us. And this battle is not one we rise to fight on rare occasions. We fight this battle daily until Jesus Christ enacts His victorious and final defeat over Satan. And as we wait for the day of Christ's return to fight the final battle, we must not for a moment let our guards down, lest we become vulnerable to Satan's schemes.

When God cursed the ground in Genesis 3 due to Adam and Eve's disobedience in eating from the Tree of Knowledge of Good and Evil, the created order of life turned upside down. Still today, chaos and disorder present themselves to us in the shadow of that curse. We misplaced our desires and affections, our hearts grew deceptive, and our inclinations became sinful. But not only was mankind affected by the fall—everything else was affected as well. Winds accelerated to speeds that could destroy. Wild animals became predators that could devour. Systems fell to corruption. As we look around us, this world and everything in it lies groaning and longing to be redeemed and restored. And while we cannot avoid the realities of the curse and its pitfalls, we must walk in faithfulness with God. We must grow in awareness of the faults and flaws of the world so that they cannot manipulate or deceive us. We must arise each day with thoughtfulness and discernment of the Lord's instruction.

Additionally, we must not diminish the reality that Satan is wholly against us. Satan introduced himself as a crafty deceiver in the garden of Eden (Genesis 3), and he continues to deceive us today. He takes advantage of every opportunity to turn us away from God to indulge in sin. His devices should never be underestimated. He is the epitome of evil and knows just what it will take to craft the temptations that curb our selfish desires and lure us into sin. Though he cannot force us to choose anything against our own will, he will do anything to make sin as enticing as possible. We must remain ready and alert for His relentless schemes.

Christians are not exempt from the temptations and consequences of sin. However, neither are we left for sin to crush us. We must never grow naive to sin, nor should we diminish the damage it causes. Instead, through salvation in Jesus Christ, He equips us to fight the battle against sin and evil from every angle. He empowers us through His great might and strength to turn away from ungodliness and pursue righteousness instead. Through a relationship with Christ, He saves us from sin and death, giving us freedom and life in its place. We are no longer representatives of ourselves but representatives of Christ, equipped in a way that is both pleasing and honorable to God as we fight the battle of sin before us. Yet we do not fight in our own strength. The Holy Spirit helps us wrestle against our sinful inclinations, the distortions of creation, and every deceptive lie Satan throws our way. We can walk forward without fear and with confidence each day as we seek the Lord in the truth of His Word.

As we step into this study, we will identify specific ways God intentionally cares for and protects us by equipping us with the armor of God. Some may be more familiar with this armor than others, but our hope is to offer a fresh perspective. As we put on the armor of God for spiritual battle, we must fight both defensively and offensively against sin. God grow us in wisdom and preparation for battle. As we aim to love and obey Him in all things, may we fight the good fight and look forward to the day of Christ's final victory over sin.

daily questions

What is your initial understanding of the armor of God after reading Ephesians 6:10-20?

In what ways do you see the necessity to fight sin in your life? How do you find yourself preparing to fight sin?

Pray and ask God for confidence in Him and to equip you through His Word. Pray that He will work in your life to fight against sin as you dive into this study.

WEEK 1 / DAY 2

The Bible points us to our greatest hope in our fight against sin – the true and lasting strength of the Lord.

Strength in the Lord

READ EPHESIANS 6:10-11, PSALM 18

In pursuit of strength, we often look to anything *but* Christ. Perhaps this looks like gaining muscle mass, exercising our minds, or achieving difficult goals. We may even look to our own determination, endurance, or willpower. But all of the earthly pursuits we might turn to in search of strength will serve us only temporarily. Certainly, those pursuits will collapse under the pressure of sin's temptations.

So, where do we find strength for the battle before us? In Ephesians 6, Paul reminds the church of Ephesus to access spiritual strength. He reminds the people that our true enemy is spiritual, so our armor and weaponry must too be spiritual in order to stand up to those evil forces. But we cannot exercise this defense in our own strength. It must come from the Lord as He spiritually equips us to fight when we are under Satan's relentless attack. The Bible points us to our greatest hope in our fight against sin—the true and lasting strength of the Lord. Our God is more capable than any willpower, weaponry, clever schemes, or defenses we have to offer. He is the essence of strength, and when we look to Him, He will uphold us with His mighty hand (Isaiah 41:10).

Scripture often refers to the Lord's strength. The Psalms, in particular, testify to the strength of the Lord. But what does it look like to manifest this strength in our lives? Psalm 89:15-17 provides a glimpse: "Happy are the people who know the joyful shout; Lord, they walk in the light from your face. They rejoice in your name all day long, and they are exalted by your righteousness. For you are their magnificent strength; by your favor our horn is exalted." Those who continually acknowledge the Lord's presence in their lives seek to honor and please Him. God is their magnificent strength. This truth insinuates that their confidence is not within themselves or their capabilities. Instead, they rejoice in God's name and celebrate His righteousness because they know the strength and peace that is found in Him alone.

King David illustrated celebrating the Lord's righteousness in Psalm 18:1-2 when he wrote, "I love you, Lord, my strength. The Lord is my rock, my fortress, and my deliverer, my God, my rock where I seek refuge, my shield and the horn of my salvation, my stronghold." David, who witnessed great warfare in his lifetime, testified to God's helping hand of strength. He reflected on the assurance he found as God fought alongside him, not only in physical battles but spiritual battles as well. David shared his confidence in knowing that we can only find true and final victory in Christ.

Through salvation in Jesus Christ, we gain access to live in God's strength. We have hope to face any battle, temptation, or trial because our God is greater than anything or anyone we face. It does not mean we will receive our desired outcome in every situation, but God will be with us, and He will not allow the weight of this world to crush us. When we are overwhelmed, burdened, or afraid, we can trust in Him for strength because He possesses and displays perfect power. He formed the earth and brought it into motion. The winds and waves obey Him. All things are held together and sustained by Him. He does what most astounds us—He holds the power of life and death. And we gain access to this same power that raised Jesus Christ from the dead when we put our hope and faith in Him—not that *we* perform such miracles, but we experience that power of Christ in our lives as we overcome battles through His strength alone and as He raises us from death to life in Him. Do you know of greater power? We see the truth of the power we hold in Roman 8:11 when Paul writes, "And if the Spirit of him who raised Jesus from the dead lives in you, then he who raised Christ from the dead will also bring your mortal bodies to life through his Spirit who lives in you." What a great hope to remember when we are tempted to stop walking forward in faith. God is not far off, but He is a near and present help in times of trouble, equipping us to do all that He has called us to do (Psalm 46:1).

As we look to God for strength and help, we can be confident that He equips us. Though weak on our own, He provides us inexhaustible strength in Himself. He instructs us to put on the full armor of God so that we can stand against the schemes of Satan. This armor is not something we can conjure up on our own. It must be given to us by God. Likewise, the armor is upheld not by our own might but by God's. However, putting on this armor requires action on our part. We are not to passively walk through life hoping in God's strength as we neglect the very means He gives to access it. Instead, we must study God's Word to learn how to wisely use the armor entrusted to us through salvation in Jesus. Scripture will aid us by increasing our awareness of our sin, growing our discernment and wisdom to fight our sin, and allowing us to rest in gospel truth. All of our "putting on" must ultimately be undergirded by trusting in the strength of the Lord. We find all assurance, not in ourselves but in Him.

God is their magnificent strength.

daily questions

Read Psalm 18:1-2, Psalm 27:1, Psalm 28:7, Psalm 89:16-17, and Psalm 118:13-14. How do these verses describe the strength of the Lord?

What does it look like for us to live in God's strength?

How does the strength of the Lord give us confidence when we feel weak and weary in the battle against sin?

WEEK 1 / DAY 3

And though this world with devils filled should threaten to undo us; We will not fear, for God has willed His truth to triumph through us.

"A Mighty Fortress is our God"

Know Your Enemy

READ EPHESIANS 6:12

Sun Tzu lived during a tumultuous time in China and authored a book called, *The Art of War*. Focusing on ancient Chinese military strategies and tactics, he wrote about the philosophies and essential strategies, not only for warfare but also for life. The phrase "know your enemy" is coined from his writing. He wrote, "It is said that if you know your enemies and know yourself you will not be put at risk even in a hundred battles. If you only know yourself, but not your opponent, you may win or may lose. If you know neither yourself nor your enemy, you will always endanger yourself." This philosophy holds great truth, especially regarding the understanding of our enemy's tactics, strategies, and schemes.

We will witness many evils of mankind—corrupt leadership, human trafficking, murder, manipulation, abuse, and other actions of those consumed by darkness. Though man's evil actions will provoke and challenge us, these actions are not the worst of our enemies. Ephesians 6:12 tells us that our fight is not against flesh and blood but against rulers, authorities, cosmic powers of darkness, evil, and spiritual forces in the heavens. The battle before us is not a fight simply against man but against that which is much more powerful. Man serves only as a pawn to stronger forces that vary in ranks and categories of evil in this world. Though we fall into the temptation of minimizing what is unseen, Satan and his demons are a very real presence that avidly works against us.

Satan means "adversary," and Scripture describes him frequently. These descriptions depict who he truly is and what he is capable of doing. He is called "the serpent" in the garden of Eden (Genesis 3:1, 14), which speaks of his crafty and cunning nature. He is referenced several times in the New Testament as "the devil," meaning "slanderer" (Matthew 4:1, 13:39, Revelation 12:9, 20:2). He is called "ruler of this world" (John 12:31, 14:30, 16:11), "the god of this age" (2 Corinthians 4:4), and "the evil one" (Matthew 13:19, 1 John 2:13).

Satan's influence is profound, and we should not ignore it. He daily orchestrates evil in pursuit of turning others away from God and His goodness. His demons are evil and delight in Satan's bidding. Satan and his demons are opposed to all that is holy and good, adhering to no moral obligation. Paul reiterated their cunning nature by exhorting the church not to fall victim to their many lies and temptations. They are sly, knowing our faults and flaws and awaiting the very moment we are most weak and susceptible to believe them. Even so, we do not fear Satan and these demons. Instead, we find encouragement to be on guard against their schemes. For this reason, 1 Peter 5:8 calls us to "Be sober-minded, be alert" as our "adversary the devil is prowling around like a roaring lion, looking for anyone he can devour."

Though we cannot stand up to the lures of sin on our own, with Jesus Christ, we can. He is our only hope in this life. The opening chapters of the Bible foretell His victorious defeat over Satan when Moses explains, "So the Lord God said to the serpent: 'I will put hostility between you and the woman, and between your offspring and her offspring. He will strike your head, and you will strike his heel'" (Genesis 3:15). God promised that, eventually, the serpent would bruise the heel of the woman's offspring, which is Jesus Christ, but Jesus would crush Satan's head. This verse brings shining hope as the first promise of a Redeemer.

Genesis 3:15 is the beginning of a long line of prophecies concerning the Promised One, who would be born to the Virgin Mary, the seed of Eve. The serpent would strike the woman's offspring, Jesus Christ—the Savior of the World. This strike would come through His crucifixion on the cross, yet "striking the heel" suggests that Jesus's pain was not final. Jesus died on our behalf, bearing the wrath of God for our disobedience so that we could be united with Him again. Though wounded for us, He rose from the dead three days later, and God promises that Jesus Christ will deliver a fatal blow to the head of Satan when He returns. Revelation 20:1-10 affirms God's promise of this defeat. Christ will bind up Satan and throw him into the abyss, eventually casting him into the lake of fire as a final crushing act to declare eternal victory over him.

We can find great comfort and help in understanding our enemy through the words of the age-old hymn, "A Mighty Fortress is our God": "And though this world, with devils filled, should threaten to undo us; we will not fear, for God has willed His truth to triumph through us." Even as we come to know our enemy is great, we can be assured that "the one who is in [us] is greater than the one who is in the world." (1 John 4:4). Our enemy brings us to a difficult battle—we do not enter an easy fight—but we can confidently wage war against him because we know that Christ will prove victorious in the end. We will stand with Him in final victory.

> *Though on our own we cannot stand up to the lures of sin, with Jesus Christ, we can.*

daily questions

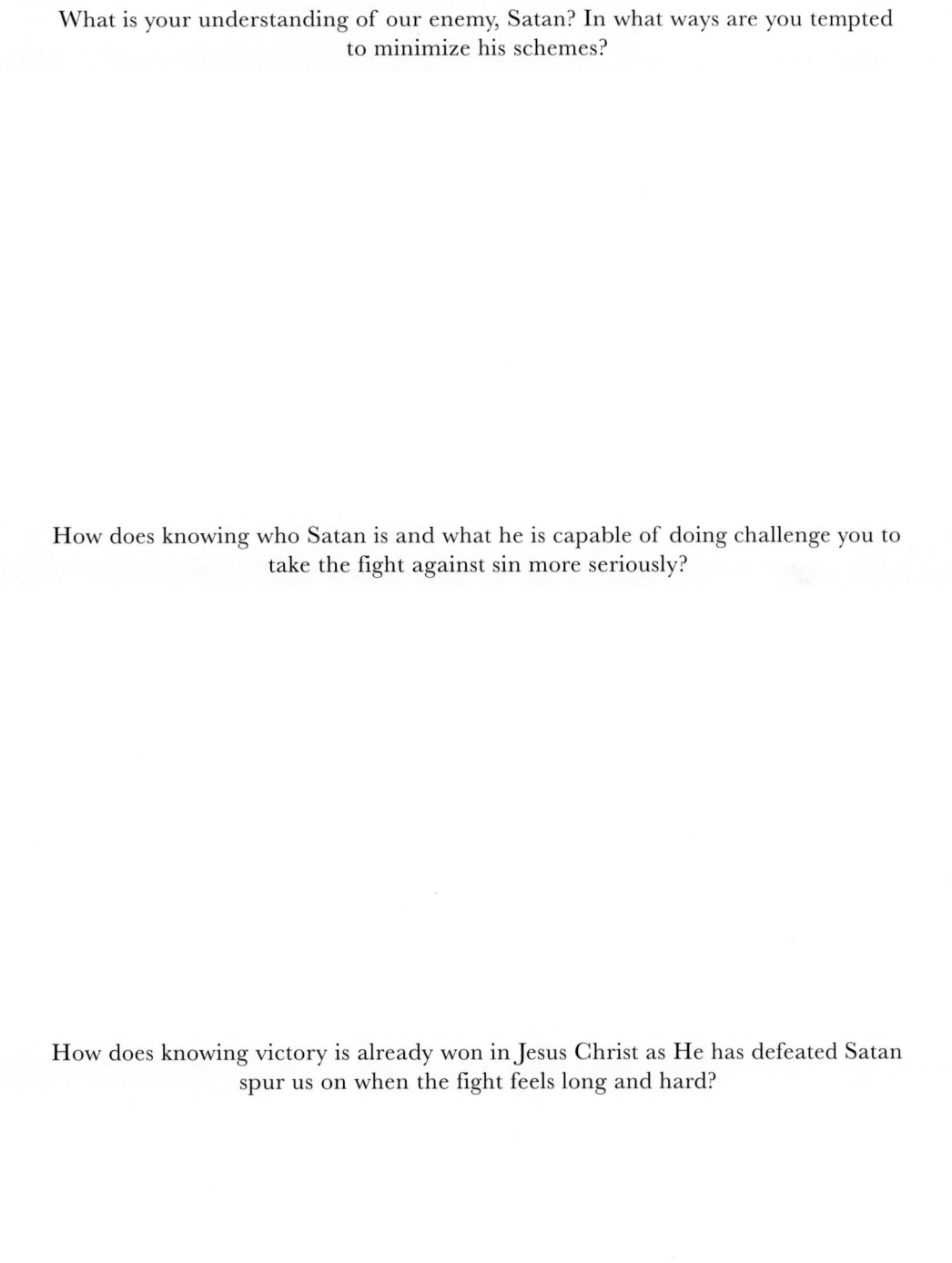

What is your understanding of our enemy, Satan? In what ways are you tempted to minimize his schemes?

How does knowing who Satan is and what he is capable of doing challenge you to take the fight against sin more seriously?

How does knowing victory is already won in Jesus Christ as He has defeated Satan spur us on when the fight feels long and hard?

WEEK 1 / DAY 4

We lack everything apart from Christ but lack no good thing in Him.

The Full Armor of God

READ EPHESIANS 6:13

The armor of God serves as the subject of a prominent passage in the New Testament. It follows the metaphor of a battle, but as mentioned before, the armor of God is not drawn from the wardrobe of the Roman soldiers but from the very nature of God. He has not simply asked us to put on the armor, but He has worn it Himself as shown in the Old Testament (Isaiah 59:12-20). He came as a great warrior and our Redeemer to execute justice against the enemies of His people, Israel. God set out to redeem and reclaim His people from the spiritual enemies of this world. What God set forth in Israel's exodus from slavery to the Egyptians, He continued through the redemptive work of His Son, Jesus, on the cross. Now, through salvation, He imparts this armor to us so that we may walk in His ways and reflect His presence in the world.

Engaging in a spiritual battle requires supernatural help outside of ourselves, and we find a hearty defense in the full armor of God (Ephesians 6:13). To understand this armor, we must first distinguish what we are to do and what God has already provided for us. The nouns presented in the passage of Ephesians each represent what God has already provided for us through Jesus Christ. The verbs shown are indicators of what we are to do. The armor of God requires a dependence on the Lord for strength and provision but also a readiness and willingness to take action. We cannot passively take up the armor of God. Rather, we must actively lean into the protection God has provided for us through it.

When we receive the gift of salvation through Jesus Christ, we are clothed with His righteousness, power, and strength (Galatians 3:27), which we receive as a gift of grace by God through faith and no contribution of our own (Ephesians 2:8-10). Our response should be to receive this gift by putting on and walking in the ways God has instructed us in His Word.

We see more evidence of this concept of "putting on" in Ephesians 4:22-24, which calls Christians "to take off your former way of life, the old self that is corrupted by deceitful desires, to be renewed in the spirit of your minds, and to put on the new self, the one created according to God's likeness in righteousness and purity of the truth." We must put off our old selves and our former ways of living in order to be clothed in Christ. Doing so requires genuine repentance on a regular basis, which means we confess our sins to the Lord and those we wrong and ask for forgiveness. Failing to change from our old ways would be like placing our finest clothes over filthy, smelly rags. Though outwardly we might look pleasant and well, the stench would overpower anyone who came close. 2 Corinthians 5:17 showcases such a transformation: "Therefore, if anyone is in Christ, he is a new creation; the old has passed away, and see, the new has come!" We become clean slates, ready to take up the armor of God. We must be willing to relinquish our efforts, our striving, our strength, and instead humbly receive the gracious gift of salvation in Jesus Christ, who promises to prepare us for the battle.

The armor of God includes the belt of truth, the breastplate of righteousness, sandals fitted in the gospel of peace, the shield of faith, the helmet of salvation, and the sword of the Spirit. This is the complete package, wrapped up in the power and provision of Christ. We lack everything apart from Christ but lack no good thing in Him. Everything He provides for us serves a specific purpose in the fight we face every day. Each piece of armor serves us purposefully to accomplish God's will.

Prayer is a final weapon that guards the entirety of our armor so that it may withstand every blow. Through Christ, we have access to God in prayer. Prayer displays our vital understanding that the armor comes from God and not ourselves. We cannot fight this battle alone. We can cry out to God for help and provision when we become weak and afraid. Just as the Psalmist proclaims, "I sought the Lord and He answered me and rescued me from all my fears" (Psalm 34:4). As we put on the armor of God, we can have confident assurance that we have protection. It is likely because we have let our guard down, pulled off the armor, or misused our weaponry that we find ourselves in spiritual defeat. Though evil awaits us at every corner, we must not forget who ultimately wins the war. When we are in Christ, Jesus equips us in His strength to fight sin as we have hope and know that He has already defeated evil once and for all.

Over the remainder of this study, we will look to Scripture to identify each piece of armor and how we are instructed to use it. Our hope is that you will feel equipped and encouraged for the daily fight against sin and evil. May you walk forward in faith without fear and with hope for the victories found in Jesus Christ.

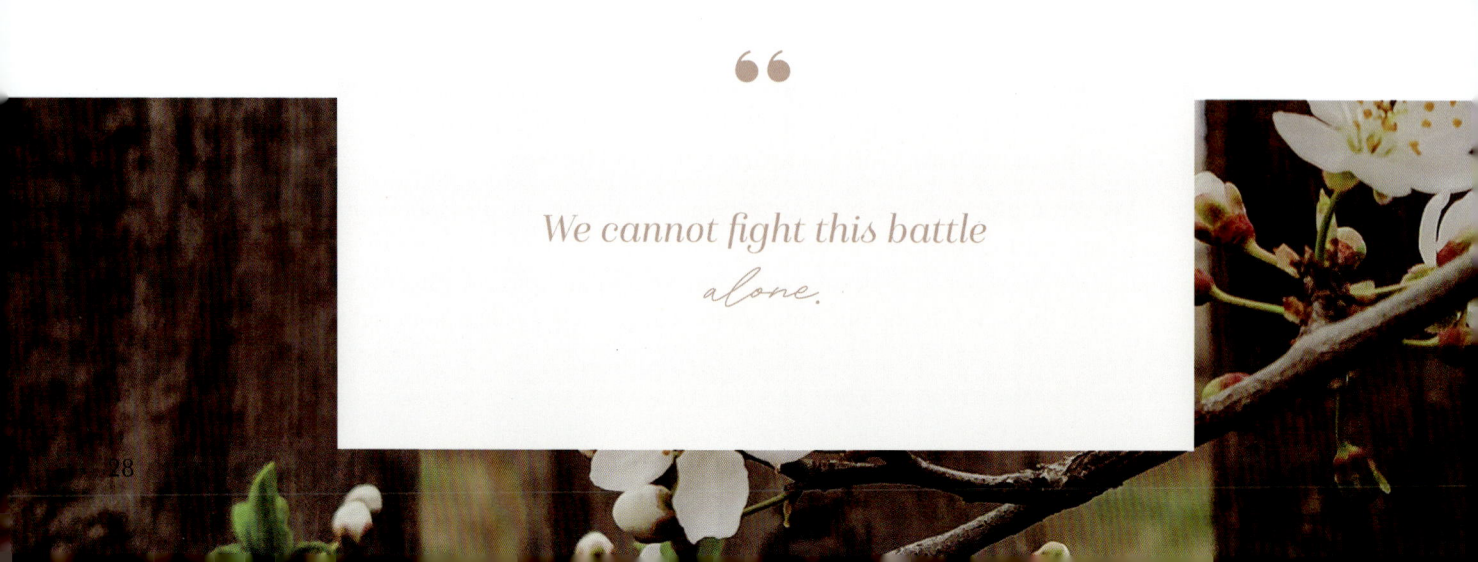

"

We cannot fight this battle alone.

daily questions

Read Isaiah 59:12-20. How do you see God instituting the armor for Himself?

How does God impart the armor to us?

In what ways have you found yourself weak under the weight of sin? What comfort do you find in knowing you do not have to conjure up your own armor in the battle against evil?

WEEK 1 / DAY 5

It is undeniably necessary to arm ourselves in God's truth as we face the fight against sin every day.

The Belt of Truth

READ EPHESIANS 6:14

When we think of armor for battle, we might not first think of a belt. However, in ancient Roman battles, the belt was a thick strap around the waist intended to hold a sheath for the sword. It was essentially a pocket for a soldier's most vitally important weapons. Additionally, strips of armor hung from it along the lower part of the body as a means of protection. If the belt was not securely fastened, a soldier's sword might fall out of place. If the belt slid off or fell sideways at any point, it might not protect from a fatal blow at the hands of the enemy. This belt held a soldier's equipment, ropes, food rations, and anything else he needed to carry. It is certainly not a piece to overlook.

In the same regard, the belt of truth is essential for us. Ephesians 6:14 tells us to stand with truth as a belt around the waist. The surrounding culture can often present the truth as something that is subjective, claiming that each person's truth is different and subject to opinion. But the Bible makes it clear that there is only one source of truth. Isaiah prophesied about a coming King who would wear righteousness and faithfulness like a belt around His waist (Isaiah 11:5). This King would hold fast to the truth of God in a way that every other king failed to do. Jesus Christ, the promised King, is *the* truth (John 14:6), meaning there is only one truth. Jesus gives us access to truth by personally revealing the Word of God to us. Every promise, purpose, and plan is brought forth in Jesus. He brought every truth to life during His time on Earth by enacting every instruction, obeying every command, loving perfectly, teaching truthfully, and walking faithfully. Because of Him, we now look to the pages of the Bible with profound hope. He lived the words He instructed us to live.

It is undeniably necessary to arm ourselves in God's truth as we face the fight against sin every day. Knowing God's truth serves as a stronghold for our hearts and minds when sin creeps in and tempts us to believe lies. The origins of sin came as a result of believing a half-truth. When God made Adam, He placed him in the garden of Eden and said, "You are free to eat from any tree of the garden, but you must not eat from the tree of the knowledge of good and evil, for on the day you eat from it, you will certainly die" (Genesis 2:16-17). This was a command Adam and Eve were to obey, not just in part but in whole.

But when the serpent appeared, ever so cunning and sly, he tempted Eve with a challenge to God's command: "Did God really say 'You can't eat from any tree in the garden'?" (Genesis 3:1). Eve responded, saying, "We may eat the fruit from the trees in the garden. But about the fruit of the tree in the middle of the garden, God said, 'You must not eat it or touch it, or you will die.'" As Adam stood with her, he could have easily encouraged her in God's command, directing her away from the tree and reminding her that God had given them everything they needed. But he did not, and they both acted sinfully in light of what they wanted to believe was true — that God was withholding good from them — instead of believing what God said. Both ate of the tree, and in turn, sin and death entered the world and fell upon all of God's creation.

God's truth serves as the basis for which we find the strength to get up each day and fight against the temptations of sin. Half-hearted attempts to know what God says to be true make us more susceptible to misunderstanding Him, or worse, disregarding His Word. Standing firm in who God says He is and what He says He will do is the only secure and solid foundation for us to stand up against Satan, "the father of lies" (John 8:44). Satan will twist the truth just enough for us to stumble into sin, just as Adam and Eve did in the garden of Eden. But with the Belt of Truth secured and fastened, we can remain unwavering and untouched by his antics. Although initially, the belt may seem insignificant, it holds the whole armor of God together. The truth of God crushes every lie of this world. May you cling to it as if your life depends on it, for assuredly, it does.

> *Every promise, purpose, and plan is brought forth in Jesus.*

daily questions

What is your understanding of truth? In what ways are you tempted to make truth dependent on your own opinion?

What are practical ways you can guard yourself against misunderstanding or disregarding God's truth?

How does knowing and believing what God says to be true equip us to fight sin?

Day 5 / 33

> The truth of God crushes every lie
> of this world. May you cling to it
> as if your life depends on it,
> for assuredly, it does.

Scripture Memory

Ephesians 6:10-13

Finally, be strengthened by the Lord and by his vast strength.

Put on the full armor of God so that you can stand against the schemes of the devil.

For our struggle is not against flesh and blood, but against the rulers, against the authorities, against the cosmic powers of this darkness, against evil, spiritual forces in the heavens.

For this reason take up the full armor of God, so that you may be able to resist in the evil day, and having prepared everything, to take your stand.

Weekly Reflection
EPHESIANS 6:10-14

Paraphrase the passage from this week.

What did you observe from this week's text about God and His character?

What do this week's passage reveal about the condition of mankind and yourself?

How does this passage point to the gospel?

How should you respond to this passage? What specific action steps can you take this week to apply this passage?

Write a prayer in response to your study of God's Word. Adore God for who He is, confess sins that He revealed in your own life, ask Him to empower you to walk in obedience, and pray for anyone who comes to mind as you study.

WEEK 2 / DAY 1

A desire to walk in accordance with God's Word provides protective parameters for life in this world.

Breastplate of Righteousness

READ EPHESIANS 6:14, ISAIAH 59:12-21

The second piece of armor that Paul brings to light is the breastplate of righteousness. During this time, Roman soldiers wore a breastplate as an essential piece of armor, which protected the chest and vital organs, so this would have been another familiar piece of armor for Paul's audience. This piece of armor was typically made of iron or bronze. Many pieces of metal overlapped to connect the front to the back, while round pieces served to protect the shoulders. The breastplate usually hung from the shoulders and rested on the hips. The overlapping pieces allowed for mobility and flexibility, so a soldier was not walking around like a tin man during battle. This important piece of armor provided defense for the heart and lungs of a soldier. If the enemy lunged with a sword, the breastplate could protect the vital organs from being punctured, which could save the soldier's life.

Righteousness brings significant defense against the attacks of the evil one. We read in Ephesians 6:14 that we are to wear it "like armor on your chest." It serves as our breastplate, our shield. Proverbs 11:4-6 assures us of its protection: "Wealth is not profitable on a day of wrath, but righteousness rescues from death. The righteousness of the blameless clears his path, but the wicked person will fall because of his wickedness. The righteousness of the upright rescues them, but the treacherous are trapped by their own desires." To be righteous means being in perfect standing with God, blameless, and walking in obedience. Scripture affirms, "Happy are those…who practice righteousness at all times" (Psalm 106:3). However, this does not mean we will always feel happy by the world's definition of the term, for we still face trials of many kinds, even as we walk with the Lord. Yet as we trust Him and walk in His ways, the Lord blesses us—He strengthens us and gives us grace upon grace through every season. Our happiness must be founded in Christ alone, and it is there we find true joy in what He did for us on the cross so that we could receive His righteousness.

Paul draws the reference of the breastplate of righteousness from the description of the Lord, our divine warrior, in Isaiah 59:17-20. This Old Testament chapter holds a description of God's promise to His people, Israel, to deal with sin, the enemy of their souls. God requires obedience. Israel disobeyed, turned away from God, sought idols and worthless things, and deserved the wrath of God. Their iniquities separated them from God and gratified the schemes of their greatest adversary. They were incapable of delivering themselves, and they should not only have been defeated but should have faced the wrathful judgment of God. Yet the Lord fought for their righteousness. He made a promise to defeat sin and bring redemption. A promise of a righteous Savior was given—a sacrifice would be made on behalf of God's unrighteous people. He would sacrifice His one and only Son, who would suffer the wrath of God as payment for the people's sin.

This redemption is offered to us as well. Our inclination toward sin gets in the way of our desires for living a perfectly upright life. We are imperfect people, like the Israelites, and we fall short of God's standard of perfection when we stand upon our own merits. Our righteousness is as filthy rags (Isaiah 64:6). So, how can we put on the breastplate of righteousness in the way Ephesians 6 calls us to do? God made a way for us to put on this righteousness through faith in His Son, Jesus Christ: "He made the one who did not know sin to be sin for us, so that in him we might become the righteousness of God" (2 Corinthians 5:21). He attributes His righteousness to those who place their faith in Him, for He took our sin upon Himself on the cross. There, in our place, Jesus bore the wrath of God for our unrighteousness. But God also makes a way for us to live out that righteousness by making us more into the likeness of Jesus as we grow in Him and in our faith. Therefore, we see righteousness in two ways: positional and conditional. Positional righteousness comes through salvation and affirms that we have been saved through faith—not by our own works—and raised to walk in the newness of life with Christ. Conditional righteousness comes through sanctification (the process of becoming Christlike) and God's recreating us into the image of Jesus by changing, shaping, and enabling us by the power of the Holy Spirit to imitate Jesus. This conditional righteousness pours out of our lives as an overflow of our positional righteousness.

Our positional righteousness secures a place for us in eternity with God, while our conditional righteousness equips us in our Christian walk on earth. Satan will attack both elements. He is our greatest accuser, and he will capitalize on every possible moment to condemn us for our unrighteousness and lead us to doubt our positional righteousness before God. Furthermore, he will lead us to doubt God's work in our lives and aim to redirect our efforts away from daily growth into the likeness of Christ. We must cling to the belt of truth to remind ourselves of what God says to be true.

We must hold fast to the truth that our righteousness is secure through the life, death, and resurrection of Jesus Christ—His life for ours. This great exchange equips us to live out His righteousness. In doing so, we are called to reflect our new identity as Christians, desiring obedience and walking in faithfulness unto the Lord. Such a pursuit serves as a great insult to Satan and blesses us in our daily efforts.

A desire to walk in accordance with God's Word provides protective parameters for life in this world. Scripture instructs us to follow in the footsteps of Christ, the One who daily defeats sin and teaches us to say "no" to ungodliness and worldly passions. He instructs us to live upright, self-controlled, and godly lives (Titus 2:12). The Lord equips us to fight against the seemingly small, everyday temptations, asking that we place our hope in the One who has also been tempted and overcome those temptations. God knows best how to fight and flourish in the world He created for us. He knows best how to prepare us for the battle. In doing so, He does not leave us with a faulty protection of our own best efforts, but through faith in Christ, He adorns us with a perfect breastplate of righteousness.

daily questions

Why is our personal righteousness not good enough? Where do we find true righteousness?

Explain the difference between positional and conditional righteousness.

What does it look like to live in light of Christ's righteousness imputed to you? How does this help you to fight sin in your life?

WEEK 2 / DAY 2

It is the gospel that returns us to a harmonious union with God.

Sandaled with Readiness for the Gospel of Peace

READ EPHESIANS 6:15

Imagine rugged terrains, long marches, and unpredictable battleground conditions. A supportive shoe would be necessary to protect a soldier's feet from disease and ruin. During the Roman Empire, walking was a primary means of transportation, so the ability to remain easily and comfortably mobile was very important. Roman soldiers wore shoes called caligae. These shoes had multiple layers of leather with straps that tied around the ankles. Additionally, the shoemaker drove pikes and iron nails through the soles of the shoes. This vital shoe design provided firm footing for soldiers in battle on unstable terrains.

In this passage, Paul encourages Christians to put on sandals with readiness for the gospel of peace. Because of sin, peace between God and men is broken. Sin creates disordered and dysfunctional relationships in the world and encourages misplaced hope and identity. It leaves us searching for resolution and comfort outside of God. Jesus Christ, however, came to serve as our mediator who would bridge the chasm created by our sin as He offered Himself in our place to restore what was broken. We receive restoration in our relationship with God through salvation in Him because of that sacrifice. And we gain access to the hope of His coming kingdom where God's people will live purposefully in perfect harmony with Him and His people forever.

We will often fight the temptation to find our footing in things apart from Christ. This means we can be tempted to find security and stability in things other than the hope of the gospel. Those things might be our careers, finances, relationships, or anything else we cling to when the world around us feels unstable. But the truth holds that nothing outside of Christ is void of disruption and dysfunction. Nothing else can provide the lasting comfort for which we long. Peace is only born by receiving the gospel's good news. It is the gospel that returns us to a harmonious union with God.

The Bible has much to say regarding the world to come when God establishes His peace-filled kingdom with His people forever. Isaiah 2:2-4 provides a glimpse:

> In the last days the mountain of the Lord's house will be established at the top of the mountains and will be raised above the hills. All nations will stream to it, and many peoples will come and say, "Come, let us go up to the mountain of the Lord, to the house of the God of Jacob. He will teach us about his ways so that we may walk in his paths." For instruction will go out of Zion and the word of the Lord from Jerusalem. He will settle disputes among the nations and provide arbitration for many peoples. They will beat their swords into plows and their spears into pruning knives. Nation will not take up the sword against nation, and they will never again train for war.

Indeed, we will be tempted to find peace in what this world has to offer. Satan falsely advertises earthly pleasures to us, promising to bring us lasting comfort. But all that Satan can offer in his nicely packaged temptation is bondage and enslavement to sin. Only Jesus can offer us the true peace that we seek. Just as Jesus told the disciples, "I have told you these things so that in me you may have peace. You will have suffering in this world. Be courageous! I have conquered the world" (John 16:33). God does not promise a conflict-free life, but in Christ, we are promised comfort in Him while we wait for God to establish His true and final peace-filled kingdom.

A solid foundation in our understanding of the gospel of peace brings hope to any circumstance we may face in this lifetime and enables us to share our hope with others. Isaiah 52:7 says, "How beautiful on the mountains are the feet of the herald, who proclaims peace, who brings news of good things, who proclaims salvation, who says to Zion, 'Your God reigns!'" Our foundation—our footing—is found in the perfect peace offered through the hope of the gospel. That foundation allows us to live in and move toward others in light of that hope. For those around us, our lives and words serve as a testimony to the peace we have found in Christ. We can point them to the only One who offers us true comfort and rest. The gospel message is a message of peace that speaks into every broken part of this world. In seasons of hardship or suffering, brokenness or doubt, fear or stress, the gospel serves as an anchor for our souls, keeping us firmly planted in the peace of Jesus. Therefore, we can walk forward in faith, ready for the wind and waves of life that come our way, because Christ, with His life, has purchased our peace.

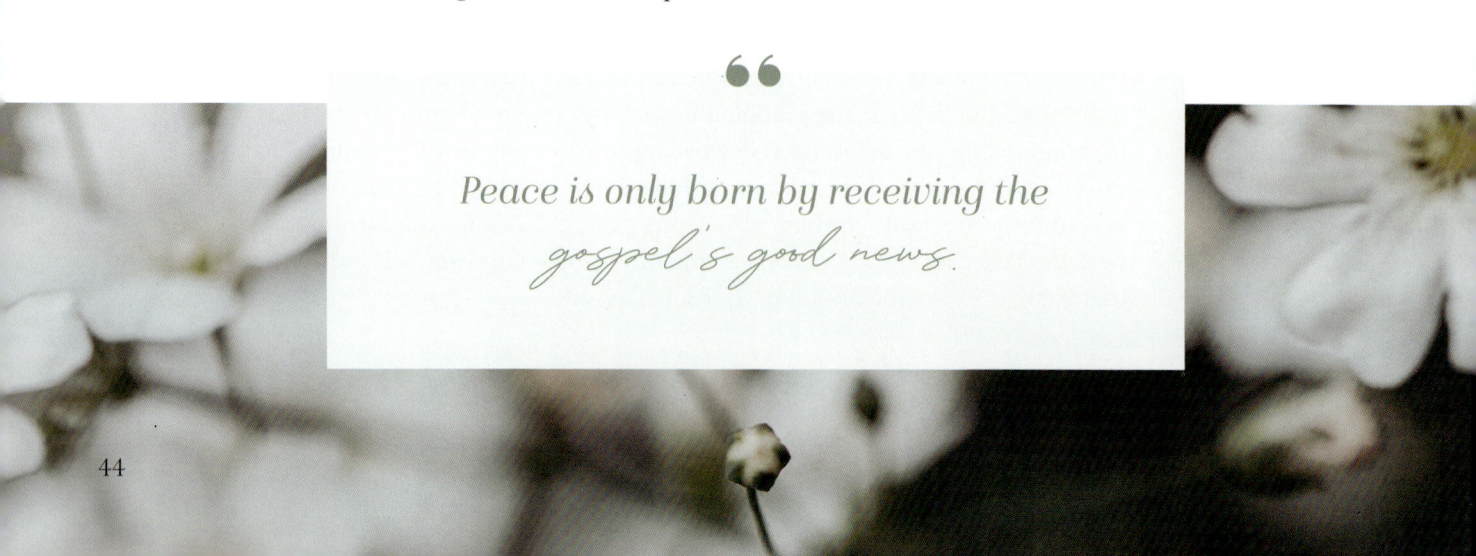

> *Peace is only born by receiving the gospel's good news.*

daily questions

How was the peace of this world broken, and how is it restored?

Where might you be tempted to find peace outside of Jesus Christ? How have you found true peace in the message of the gospel?

How does the gospel message of peace equip you in the fight against sin and brokenness?

WEEK 1 / DAY 3

Faith is the realization of our hope gained through salvation and a firm belief in God's promises to us.

Shield of Faith

READ EPHESIANS 6:16

A Roman shield, called a *scutum*, weighed nearly 22 pounds and could protect a majority of one's body. These shields were often rectangular with rounded corners and made from two sheets of wood, fastened together. They were typically covered with leather and doused with water to protect the soldiers against flaming arrows and sometimes adorned with metal strips, which were used as a weapon of force. It is evident the shield was a substantial piece of armor for any soldier in battle, a fitting metaphor for Paul's exhortation to be armored in faith.

The author of Hebrews describes faith as "the reality of what is hoped for, the proof of what is not seen" (Hebrews 11:1). Faith is the realization of our hope gained through salvation and a firm belief in God's promises to us. From the opening pages of the Bible, God made a promise to rescue His people from sin. Through generations and generations, this promise was brought forth and realized in Jesus Christ. Though men and women in the Old Testament looked forward in faith to the coming Messiah, Christians now look back in faith to the cross upon which the Messiah gave His life. Those men and women never witnessed the full culmination of that promise in their lifetime, yet their faith assured them because they were offered a future hope. We know God brought a Savior just as He said He would. And although we did not see our Savior with our own eyes as He walked this earth, our faith assures us about that which we have not yet seen.

Taking up the shield of faith means trusting in God's provision and promises. God is our great protector and provider. But we are prone to doubt Him. When our circumstances are hard and difficult, we may wish for God to provide instant escape or clear answers. Maybe Satan tempts us to give in to his lies and indulge in sin, having us believe there is something better for us. But we must acknowledge our weak and wandering eyes and use our faith as a shield of protection. While Satan over promises and under delivers, faith reminds us that God is true and trustworthy, and He has a perfect record of keeping His promises to us. God calls us to walk forward in faith, even when we cannot see how He is at work (2 Corinthians 5:7). God is a warrior on our behalf, keeping us from being destroyed by Satan's attacks. We are guarded against the death and destruction caused by sin through Jesus's sacrifice for us on the cross. But we are also led forward and shielded from temptation to sin on a daily basis with the help of the Holy Spirit, who is at work in us and teaches us to walk in holiness.

What preservation we find through faith in Jesus Christ! Unwavering faith guards us against the flaming arrows of doubt, fear, and hopelessness that Satan throws our way, and it leads us to stand before the throne of God, unblemished by his many throws. By grace through faith, we are saved from our sins and justified. God brings us into His family to live in His presence forever, for in Christ's death, justice was served. Christ absorbed the blows of Satan through His death and emerged victorious in His resurrection. We will lose the battle if left to ourselves. But through faith in Christ, we find hope in a better outcome. Faith leads us to persevere. We are no longer exposed and unprotected but are walking forward into the battle of sin with confident hope that God will bring us to the other side. No matter the discouragement, suffering, shortcomings, doubts, or disappointments this life brings, may we not shrink back. God can use anything as a means of bringing us closer to Himself. He equips us so that we will never be crushed by the flaming arrows thrown in our direction. Our faith may waiver, but God is perfecting our faith every single day as He provides opportunities for us to fully trust in Him.

We will join the saints of old one day, and our faith will be visible as we witness the culmination of God's promises in full—when He returns to vanquish evil and calls us home to eternal glory with Him. We will see victory over sin if we stay the course, for our faith will shield us from disbelief and doubt. We will see the victorious defeat over Satan that we read about in the first few chapters of Genesis, and we will stand with Christ in final victory: "...everyone who has been born of God conquers the world. This is the victory that has conquered the world: our faith" (1 John 5:4).

> *God can use anything as a means of bringing us closer to Himself.*

daily questions

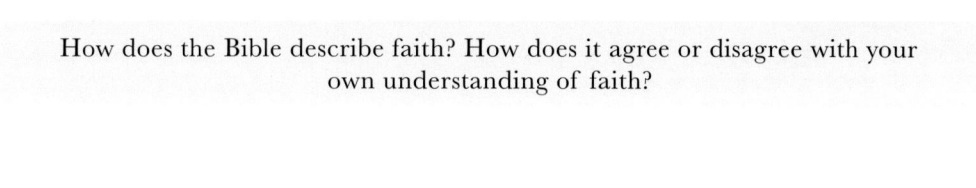

How does the Bible describe faith? How does it agree or disagree with your own understanding of faith?

What does it mean to put on the shield of faith? How does faith help us to fight sin?

What does it mean that one day our faith will be made visible?

WEEK 2 / DAY 4

What a beautiful inheritance awaits God's people on the other side of every difficulty and temptation we face in this life.

Helmet of Salvation

READ EPHESIANS 6:17

Alongside the breastplate of righteousness, the helmet of salvation is derived from Isaiah 59:17 and is a piece of armor that God wears Himself. Salvation and righteousness are referenced together many times throughout Scripture because the righteous requirement of God is satisfied completely in Jesus Christ so that salvation can be offered freely to the unrighteous. We have no access to righteousness without salvation in Jesus Christ. Neither do we have righteousness on our own. If God were to deal with us accordingly, we would be recipients of His wrath and judgment. But God deals with us in the same way He dealt with a rebellious Israel. Isaiah reveals that God would not send His wrathful judgment to His people. Instead, He would send His only Son to bring salvation near.

The imagery of a helmet emphasizes the head. Of course, in any form of battle, protection for the head against flying bullets or other fatal blows was of great necessity. It is typical, even today, for military men to wear a protective helmet of sorts. In Scripture, the head is often referenced as the most essential part of a person. Whether bringing a blessing (Genesis 49:26) or a curse (Ezekiel 22:31), it is said to be brought down on one's head. This is why hands are laid on one's head to bless them (Genesis 48:18) and why hands are laid on the head of an animal sacrifice for sins committed (Exodus 29:15). Therefore, it seems appropriate that the helmet in the armor of God refers to the gift of salvation.

Salvation is offered to us once and for all through Jesus Christ. When we truly come to know Him as our Lord and Savior, the Bible says no one can snatch us from His hand (John 10:28). So how do we reconcile this truth with the exhortation to put on the helmet of salvation? Is salvation something that can be put off and put on again? 1 Thessalonians 5:8 gives us further explanation for what Paul is saying: "let us be self-controlled and put on the armor of faith and love, and a helmet of the hope of salvation." Hope is a fruit of salvation in our hearts and lives. Paul encourages us to put on hope. This hope is not vague optimism or wishful thinking, but it is absolute assurance that God offers us through Jesus Christ. It is a settled and secured conviction of life in eternity after death. We find confident assurance of our hope in the finished work of Jesus on the cross. He paid the ultimate price—His life—to offer us salvation.

Through His death, He conquered the grave so that God's people, though they may die to this world, will never truly die (in the eternal sense) but will be raised to walk with Him forever (1 Thessalonians 4:16-17).

Therefore, the hope of salvation offers abundant protection and comfort in this life. We will face suffering and many kinds of trials in this lifetime. We will fall short in our obedience, and our eyes will wander to worthless idols. Satan will hurl many accusations our way in attempts to make us question our secured salvation. But even so, we are held by a living hope with an inheritance that is imperishable, undefiled, and unfading, kept in heaven for and guarded by God's power for us (1 Peter 1:3-5). Because this inheritance is sure, God is preparing us to receive it every day. He does not leave us to ourselves, but He shapes us in righteousness and obedience. He uses every opportunity to bring us to love and trust Him more. He is sanctifying us into the likeness of Christ so that "when he appears, we will be like him because we will see him as he is" (1 John 3:2).

As we walk through life, Hostility and hardship will certainly come our way. People may hurl attacks and insults in our direction, causing us to question the promises of God. We may face circumstances that make us feel like God is absent. Satan would love to fill our minds with doubt—causing us to doubt God and His promises. He would love to direct our attention elsewhere to place our hope in fleeting things. He would love to make sin an enticing escape. But we are not left to a flimsy defense against discouragement and despair. God equips us to put on the helmet of our salvation as we remember that Jesus is our hope who came to rescue His people from this world, and He will come again to make all things new. 2 Corinthians 4:16-17 says, "Therefore we do not give up. Even though our outer person is being destroyed, our inner person is being renewed day by day. For our momentary light affliction is producing for us an incomparable eternal weight of glory." What a beautiful inheritance awaits God's people on the other side of every difficulty and temptation we face in this life.

> *Hope is a fruit of salvation in our hearts and lives.*

daily questions

How do salvation and righteousness go hand in hand?

What does it mean to put on salvation?

How does the hope of salvation offer abundant protection and comfort in this life?

WEEK 1 / DAY 3

God authenticates His promise of full and final redemption by giving the Holy Spirit to indwell us.

Sword of the Spirit

READ EPHESIANS 6:17, HEBREWS 4:12

The sword of a Roman soldier was known as a *gladius*. Sharpened on both sides and the point, it could pierce through armor. This became known as one of the most fearsome and lethal weapons of the time. It is suitable that Paul uses the imagery of the sword to represent the Word of God. Hebrews 4:12 gives the same picture as it refers to God's Word as being sharper than any double-edged sword. What is important to note about this particular piece of armor is that it is the only offensive piece. The belt, breastplate, sandals, shield, and helmet are all to be used as protective gear in defense of an attack. But the sword is to be used as a weapon to pierce, penetrate, and divide.

Paul draws the example from Isaiah 49:2, which predicts the coming Messiah: "He made my words like a sharp sword; he hid me in the shadow of his hand. He made me like a sharpened arrow; he hid me in his quiver." We now know this prophecy is fulfilled in Jesus, who is the eternal Word who came in the flesh to reveal God to the world. He not only lived His life and ministry speaking the words of God, but Jesus Himself embodied all that the Scriptures say of who God is. The Bible is a gift, holding the inspired words of God intended to teach us, train us, and help us to know and love God more. God's Word holds the story of God's plan of redemption, and it holds specific instructions for how to live in light of that story. It provides words of comfort and words of strength. It heals, rebukes, challenges, and encourages us. It is a bottomless treasure to those who read from it and serves as a necessary help in the battle of spiritual warfare. It gives everything we need for the Christian life, and we need it to fight sin. We find this perfectly exemplified through Jesus when He was tempted by Satan in the wilderness (Matthew 4:1-11). Jesus responded with perfect knowledge and understanding of God's Word, reciting it as a defense against Satan's attacks every time he challenged Jesus.

Being named the sword *of the Spirit*, reveals this is not a weapon we have in and of ourselves. It is given to us. The Spirit, which is the Holy Spirit, must enable and equip us to understand the Word of God. As 1 Corinthians 2:14 informs us, "But the person without the Spirit does not receive what comes from God's Spirit, because it is foolishness to him; he is not able to understand it since it is evaluated spiritually." According to Ephesians 4:18-19, apart from salvation in Jesus Christ, our hearts are hardened and darkened from understanding the intentions and instructions of God. We are calloused and alienated from the life of God. We do not choose it. Instead, we run to gratify our selfish desires. But when we repent from our sin and place our hope and faith in Jesus, we are sealed with the Holy Spirit. What this means is that God authenticates His promise of full and final redemption by giving the Holy Spirit to indwell us. In doing so, the Holy Spirit guides, shapes, and works in us to walk in faithfulness and grow in Christlikeness in preparation for the fulfillment of that promise. The Spirit equips us to know and understand God's Word so that we may remember it and obey it.

Knowing God's Word is essential for fighting temptation and sin, and what a comfort that the Holy Spirit helps us discern and understand how to best use it. Jesus knew God's Word, and therefore, He knew how to obey it. We too can walk in obedience, with the help of the Holy Spirit, by knowing and delighting in God's Word. When idolatry looks desirable, the Bible reminds us of the destruction it brings. When sinful indulgences look to offer relief, Scripture reminds us that nothing of this world can bring us lasting comfort. God's Word points us to what is true when we are tempted to fall victim to lies. The Spirit helps us remember and discern the truth found in God's Word, even in our weakness, as we struggle to know how best to use it in our daily battle against sin. By regularly reading it, memorizing it, knowing it, and understanding it, we arm ourselves with the greatest weapon known to man, and we prepare ourselves to put His Word to use. We need the truth of God's Word readily accessible in our hearts and minds for moments when we feel caught off guard or surprised by sin. This requires a commitment to God's Word for the long haul. There will never be a day when sin is not knocking on our door, and there will never be a day when the knowledge of God's Word, enabled by the Holy Spirit, cannot fight it.

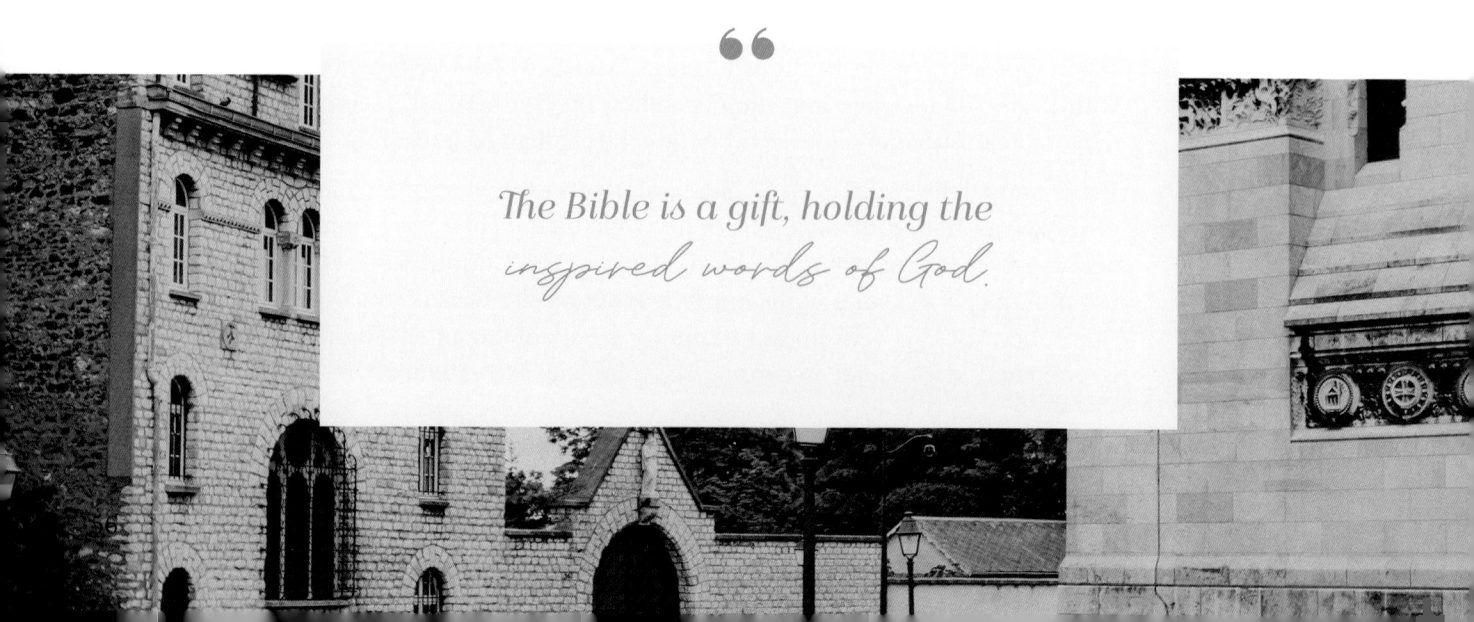

> *The Bible is a gift, holding the inspired words of God.*

daily questions

What power does the Word of God hold in our daily fight against sin?

What role does the Holy Spirit play in our understanding of God's Word?

What are practical ways you can seek to know God's Word more deeply in your life?

> There will never be a day when sin is not knocking on our door, and there will never be a day when the knowledge of God's Word, enabled by the Holy Spirit, cannot fight it.

Scripture Memory

Ephesians 6:14-17

Stand, therefore, with truth like a belt around your waist, righteousness like armor on your chest,

and your feet sandaled with readiness for the gospel of peace.

In every situation take up the shield of faith with which you can extinguish all the flaming arrows of the evil one.

Take the helmet of salvation and the sword of the Spirit—which is the word of God.

Weekly Reflection
EPHESIANS 10:14-17

Paraphrase the passage from this week.

What did you observe from this week's text about God and His character?

What do this week's passage reveal about the condition of mankind and yourself?

How does this passage point to the gospel?

How should you respond to this passage? What specific action steps can you take this week to apply this passage?

Write a prayer in response to your study of God's Word. Adore God for who He is, confess sins that He revealed in your own life, ask Him to empower you to walk in obedience, and pray for anyone who comes to mind as you study.

Weekly Reflection

WEEK 3 / DAY 1

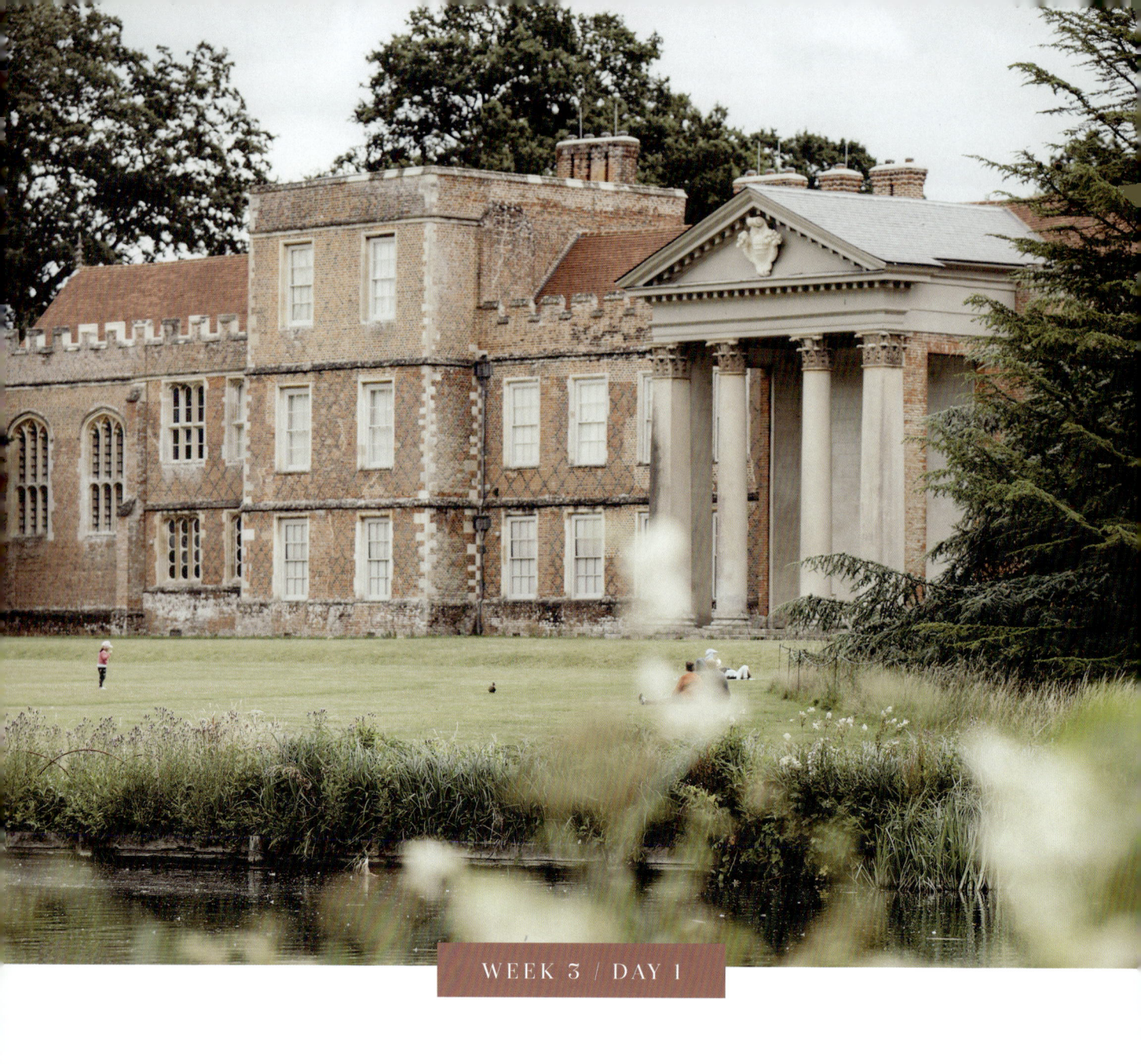

Continual prayer invites us to a constant dependence and trust in the Lord.

Devoted to Prayer

READ EPHESIANS 6:18, 1 THESSALONIANS 5:16-18

As we enter into the last week of this study, we see Paul begin to conclude his emphasis on Christian warfare and shift to the importance of an enveloping devotion to prayer. Though prayer is not a named weapon in the armor of God, it is still of great necessity in our daily battle against sin. It is a privilege, as Christians, to have access to the Father in prayer. Through Jesus Christ as our mediator, we can seek God for comfort and help when we need it most. Every branch of prayer is of great value, whether we pray against evils, petition for God's grace, or praise the Lord for His mercies. We cannot ever exhaust the access granted to us. We can humbly approach Him with our inadequacies any moment, with hope and trust in His sufficiency over our own.

With an understanding that we will face sin and temptation daily, why would we not call on God in prayer? Jesus instructs us in the Lord's Prayer in Matthew 6:13 to pray, "and do not bring us into temptation but deliver us from the evil one." We need God's help to refrain from falling into temptation. Even if we desire good, we are inclined toward our sinful nature. Our desires can tempt us to fall victim to the traps of Satan and temptations of sin. We live in a constant state of spiritual warfare. We can understand ourselves better in knowing that even if we desire to do good, we do not always do it (Romans 7:19). It is only through the intercession of the Holy Spirit and the active work of God's Word at work in our hearts that we choose to fight against temptation and sin instead of giving in to it. God equips us with His armor because He knows that temptation in this life will come, and we will not be able to fight it on our own. Furthermore, as Jesus instructed His disciples, we can pray for protection and provision from the One who has sufficient strength and power to prevail over sin.

Continual prayer invites us to constant dependence and trust in the Lord. It acknowledges that we are in need of Him every second of every day. In moments when we have trouble discerning what is true and what is not, we can pray and ask God to bring the truth of His Word to our minds. When we find ourselves in situations that taunt our weaknesses, we can pray and ask God for strength to fight against temptation. When we find ourselves looking at sin in a desirable way, we can pray and ask God to turn our eyes away from worthless things and find true delight in Him. Even if we do not know exactly what or how to pray, the Spirit will intercede for us in prayer (Romans 8:26-27).

There are countless ways we can practice prayer in a way that postures our hearts and minds toward the only One who can truly equip us for the battle against sin. Even if we find ourselves falling into sin, we can come before the Lord in prayerful repentance. We can ask for His forgiveness. We can beg Him to help us hate our sin and remind us of its consequences. We can even name specific sins we fall victim to and ask God to eradicate them from our lives. What a gift of grace that a holy God, through the mediating work of Jesus Christ, hears the prayers of lowly sinners like us. And not only does He hear us, but He delights in hearing us, and He helps us in our every moment of need.

God desires to make us holy as He is holy (1 Peter 1:16). He commands us to pursue righteousness and flee from sin. However, He does not command this without making a way to obey this command. God promises that He always provides a way for us to endure through trials and temptations (1 Corinthians 10:13). However, that does not mean He will take them away immediately or even in this lifetime. By asking the Father not to bring us to temptation, we are submitting to God's ultimate deliverance and pleading with God to spare us from the temptations and spiritual attacks of sin in everyday life. Jesus teaches us to pray for endurance and perseverance in the fight against sin. We need His help. Sin and temptation will be a lifelong battle, and we need the Lord for strength to overcome it. Daily pleading for God's protection from sin reveals a right understanding of the evils of this world and God's power and provision. We need the Lord's help to graciously guide us away from temptation at every turn, so let us not neglect Paul's exhortation to devote ourselves to prayer.

> *Through Jesus Christ as our mediator, we can seek God for comfort and help when we need it most.*

daily questions

How does Jesus model for us the way to pray against sin and temptation? How can you regularly implement these requests into your prayer life?

How does prayer equip us in the fight against sin? Why is it important to pray for God to deliver us from evil, with a secured knowledge that He will?

Write a prayer asking God to lead you away from the temptation of sin, naming specific temptations you face in your own life. Pray for deliverance to come and for God to put an end to evil once and for all.

WEEK 3 / DAY 2

Nothing can separate us from that which is promised through salvation.

Perseverance

READ EPHESIANS 6:18, GALATIANS 6:9

Consider athletes who are just beginning their sport. In their first few attempts, they often fail and fail again. They are still learning the rules and developing their skills. Growing and perfecting their skill will take time and practice, and there will likely be bumps along the way. Maybe an injury will arise, maybe they perform poorly, or maybe they receive difficult critiques. Maybe their competition proves more fierce, or they find their energy and drive to be lacking. At any time, an athlete could just throw their hands up and quit. One might question the point in continuing on in the face of difficulty. But it is often through perseverance that an athlete learns and grows in skill, becoming better and better over time.

Likewise, Christians must also grow in perseverance. Our journey begins when we open our eyes anew to the astounding truth of who God is and what He has done when we come to know Him as our Lord and Savior. He calls us to seek Him, grow in our knowledge of Him, and learn how He commands His people to live. We do so by studying God's Word, practicing prayerfulness, surrounding ourselves with other believers, and walking out our faith to a watching world. Yet our Bibles may seem initially daunting, and seeing the lives of faithful Christians around us can leave us feeling defeated.

Learning to walk in obedience can seem challenging. Using our comparison to athletes, Christians will certainly stumble along the way, but with time and perseverance, they will grow to live and love in a way that exemplifies a greater knowledge of God. In contrast to athletes, Christians are not left to simply work hard by reading their Bibles more, sinning less, and perfecting themselves. Christians are helped along in life by a divine guide, the Holy Spirit, and held secure in God's promise that because He began a good work in us, He will bring that work to full completion (Philippians 1:6).

Paul, in His closing remarks, calls the church to stay alert with perseverance. After listing the spiritual equipment provided by God to wage war in this lifetime, he wants the recipients of this letter to understand proper expectations. The armor of God does not promise a life free of difficulty, nor does it promise that we will never fall victim to sin. Instead, the armor equips us to persevere through every trial and temptation. It equips us to keep our eyes fixed ahead, not consumed by our present circumstances but looking forward to what is to come. It equips us for whatever sin struggle we may have that seems impossible to shake—whether it be an addiction, idolatry, a mental battle, a problem with anger or impatience, or a tendency to lie or gossip. Yes, we are both called and equipped to fight against those things. We must remain ready and alert to combat the lies they taunt us each day with God's steadfast and lasting truth. And as we fight, we must not lose heart.

The doctrine of perseverance teaches that all who truly find salvation in Jesus Christ will be kept by God's saving grace and will persevere as Christians until the end of their lives. Through salvation, we have assurance that God's power will carry us through this life, and we will live with Him in eternity one day (John 10:27-29). Perseverance to the end is the fruit of a genuine assurance of salvation. This confidence anchors us through any trial and temptation in this life. Nothing can separate us from that which is promised through salvation.

Perseverance in the Christian faith commits to obedience in light of the hope of Christ. It is continuing to contend for the things of God when people around us seem to belittle them. The Christian life will be hard, and there is no need to sugarcoat that truth (John 16:33). The battle against sin will often leave us staring our weaknesses in the face. Just when we feel we have conquered one area of our lives, another area rears its ugly head. We could easily find ourselves discouraged by our sin and wondering if we can truly overcome it. But the good news of the gospel reminds us that we are not purchased momentarily by the blood of Jesus, but we are purchased for glory for all of eternity. The Holy Spirit and God's Word are at work in our hearts and minds, growing us in the fruit of the Spirit, sanctifying us to hate sin and love righteousness, and leading us to pursue godliness and the glory of God in all things. God is making us new every single day, perfecting us into the likeness of Jesus. Even when we fall and feel unable to stand again, may we find the strength to persevere with the promise that God will stop at nothing to carry us to completion.

> *Perseverance to the end is the fruit of a genuine assurance of salvation.*

daily questions

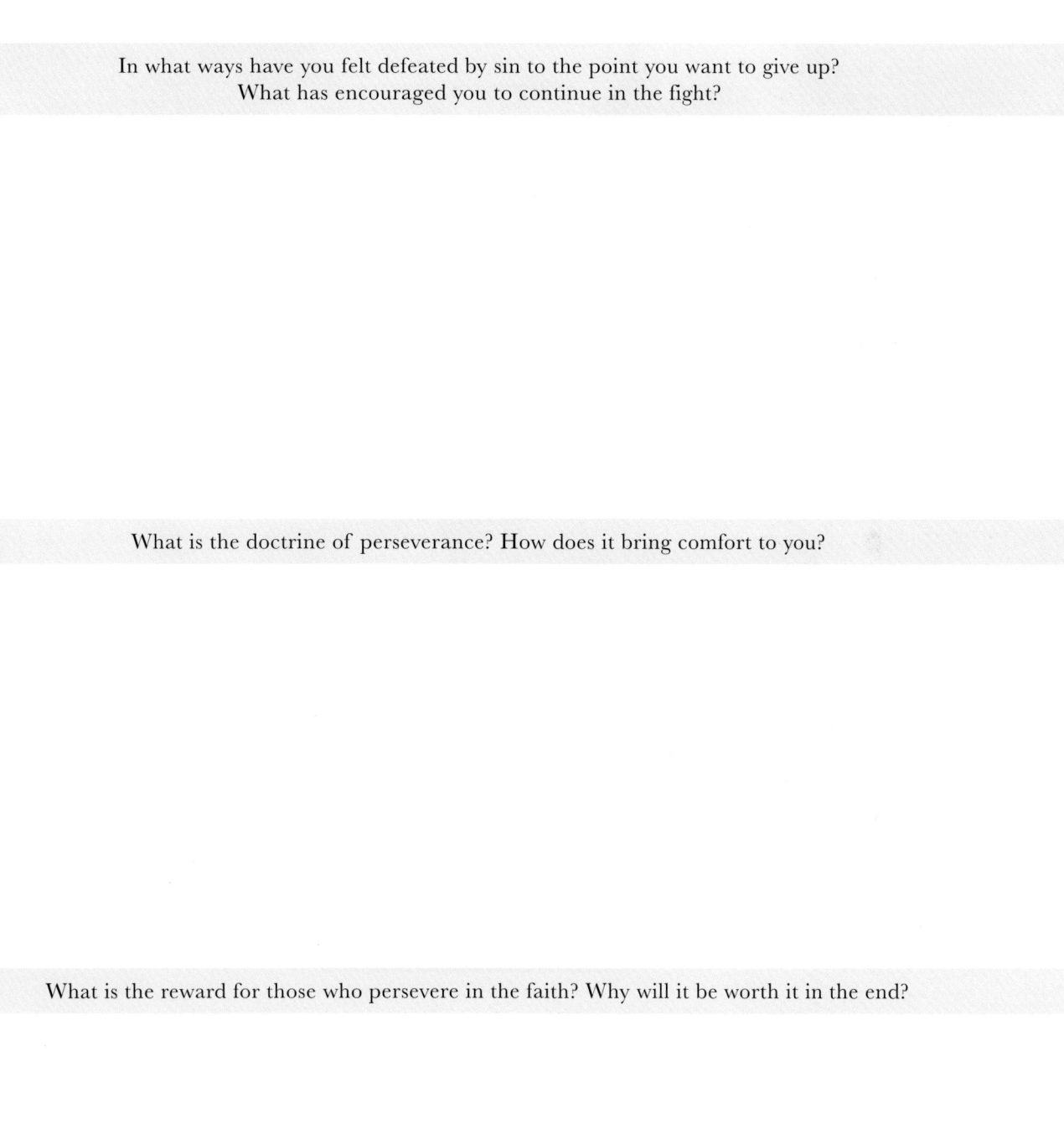

In what ways have you felt defeated by sin to the point you want to give up?
What has encouraged you to continue in the fight?

What is the doctrine of perseverance? How does it bring comfort to you?

What is the reward for those who persevere in the faith? Why will it be worth it in the end?

WEEK 3 / DAY 3

The battle against sin and temptation is not only a personal fight but a fight all Christians face together.

Intercede for the Saints

READ EPHESIANS 6:18

How many times have we seen a brother or sister of the faith fall victim to sin? How often have we committed to praying against that very sin on their behalf? How often have we prayed for our church families and other Christians to be protected against the attacks of Satan? The battle against sin and temptation is not only a personal fight but a fight all Christians face together. Satan is at war with God and all of God's people. Just as we see the importance of praying for ourselves, there is equal importance in fighting alongside one another by praying for others.

By praying for our fellow brothers and sisters in the faith, we can take deliberate action to intercede for them on their behalf. This type of intercession is encouraged throughout Scripture. The apostle Paul encouraged this same action in Ephesians 6:18, just as he did in 1 Timothy 2:1-2 when he wrote, "First of all, then, I urge that petitions, prayers, intercessions, and thanksgivings be made for everyone." Jesus accomplished the work of intercession on our behalf when He took our place on the cross. Still today, He intercedes for us with the Father and the Holy Spirit, helping us pray as we ought. So then, we reflect His compassionate and selfless nature by interceding for others. As we consider the needs of others, bear their burdens, and make requests on their behalf, we not only serve them but bring glory to God. Satan would love us to be self-focused, fight our own battles, and leave others to their own demise. However, God calls us to something greater. He calls us to be kingdom-focused, fighting sin on behalf of all God's people so that they will flourish in the faith and glorify Him.

God gives us plenty of instruction in His Word to intercede in prayer on behalf of others. One of the apostles, James, directs us to the effectiveness of praying earnestly for one another in saying that "the prayer of a righteous person is very powerful in effect" (James 5:16). He references the prayers of the prophet Elijah, who prayed earnestly that it would not rain in order to turn people away from their idol worship and back to the Lord in repentance and ultimate dependence on Him (1 Kings 18). The simple blessing of rain was leading people to complacency as they disregarded the goodness of God. So, Elijah prayed, and God answered. It did not rain for three years. And then, when the people's dependence on the Lord was strengthened, Elijah prayed for the rain to return, and God returned it.

Prayer is powerful, and when we witness others falling into sin, we can pray specifically against the temptations that entice them. If we notice friends struggling with envy and jealousy, we can pray that God would bring them to rich contentment in the lives God has given them. If we know brothers or sisters in Christ fighting lustful thoughts, we can ask God to turn them away from anything that leads their eyes to wander. If we know someone indulging in a sinful relationship, we can pray and ask God to lead that person out of it. We can do something as simple as praying for others to grow in understanding and discernment of God's Word so that they can better stand against Satan's schemes. Not only does God know better how to intervene in the lives of those battling sin, but He has the power to intervene, and He will accomplish what He sets out to do.

Interceding in prayer for others does not negate our responsibility to speak truth into their lives, encourage them, and walk faithfully alongside them. We can be tempted to pass out the encouragement, "I'm praying for you," like candy to those who share their light or large burdens with us. But let us be people who follow through with prayer and pray continually. Then let us be people who follow up and hold one another accountable as we play a part in God's redemptive work. Instead of throwing around false praise and empty comforts, let us remind one another of sin's evil and destructive nature if we continue in it. And finally, let us be people who are willing to join others in the fight. Let us join in the fight when we see others are struggling to fit themselves in the armor of God, struggling to rest in God's protection and provision, or struggling to persevere. Let us join them in the ministry of prayer and the ministry of presence. All of us limp toward heaven, and we all need help along the way. Let us be to others what we hope someone will be for us—a fellow fighter, willing to help support us, dust us off, and point us to the coming victory.

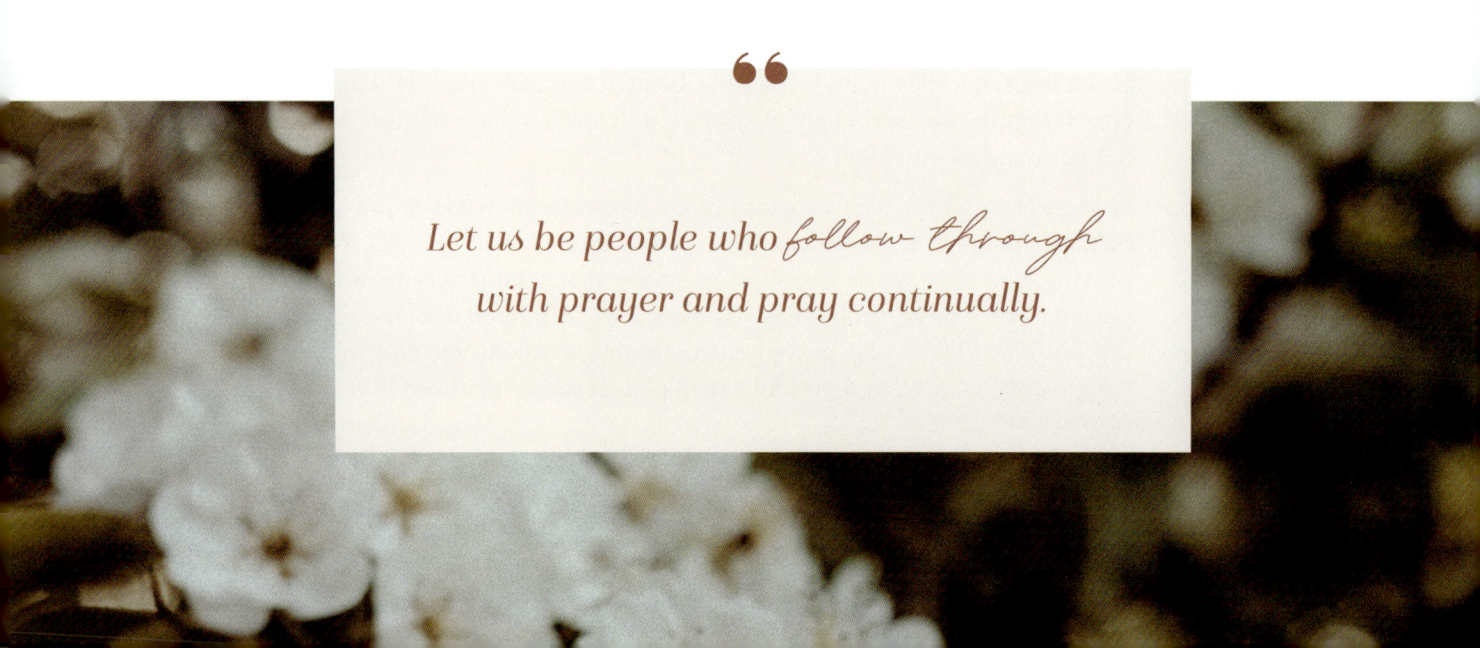

> *Let us be people who follow through with prayer and pray continually.*

daily questions

Why is the fight against sin not just personal but also communal with God's people?

How can you practice praying regularly for the specific sin struggles of others?
Can you think of a specific person you can pray for right now?

How have you seen God's redemptive work in your own life through the prayers of other Christians?

WEEK 3 / DAY 4

Though we deserve death, we have been raised to life in Christ.

The Gospel Goes Forth

READ EPHESIANS 6:19-20

A shift at the end of Paul's explanation of the armor of God is a request for the church of Ephesus to pray for him. After exhorting the church, he asks specifically that they would pray for his boldness with the gospel and that he would continue to share the message of Jesus. This shows incredible humility and credits everything he says and does to the ministry of preaching the gospel. Paul does not speak from a position of perfectly obeying the words he presents. He was a limited man, just as we are, yet his limitations did not deter him from walking forward in faith, preaching and teaching the truth of the gospel. His gracious request came from a sincere heart and desire to continue with strength and endurance in work and service to the mission of Christ.

What is important about this shift is that it reminds us that the gospel must go forth. We face our own battles against sin, but they must not consume us to such an extent that we neglect the ministry opportunities that surround us. God has entrusted us with a message that brings life from death—the message of the gospel. God the Father sent His one and only Son to die a death that we deserved so that we could take on the righteousness of Christ and live in a relationship with Him both now and forever. Though we deserve death, we have been raised to life in Christ. The beauty of the gospel is that it changes everything. It changes the way we view ourselves and others. It changes the way we speak, act, and live. It changes the purpose and pursuits of our lives. Only as recipients of the gospel can we dress ourselves each day with God's armor. God has given us access through salvation to walk in His provision and protection as we face the daily battle of spiritual warfare.

But for those who have not found salvation in Jesus Christ, they experience the horror and devastation of sin with no protection. The attacks of Satan prove successful, and their desires lead them into darkness and destruction. Only by God's common grace to mankind has everyone apart from Him not experienced a fatal blow. The battlefield for Christians and non-Christians is the same, yet Christians are given supernatural protection and weaponry to fight. Not only that, Christians fight with the promise of a secured victory. With possession of such help and hope, why would we leave our fellow image-bearers unarmed and left to die? Would we not do everything in our power to show them the hope offered through the gospel of Jesus?

Christians are called to carry the gospel message to the ends of the earth. We are not instructed to wait until we are perfect to share the hope that we have found. It is because of our imperfect nature that the message of the gospel is necessary for us. Every moment that we wait for heaven is another day God has given us to help spare someone from the evil realities of hell. 2 Peter 3:9 tells us, "The Lord does not delay his promise, as some understand delay, but is patient with you, not wanting any to perish but all to come to repentance." God graciously provides time for sinners to repent, and He has enlisted us to share the message that changes hearts and leads sinners to repentance. Paul was bound in chains and continued to share the gospel. We too can use our trials and sufferings to showcase the glory of God and the hope of our Savior to a watching world.

> *Every moment that we wait for heaven is another day God has given us to help spare someone from the evil realities of hell.*

daily questions

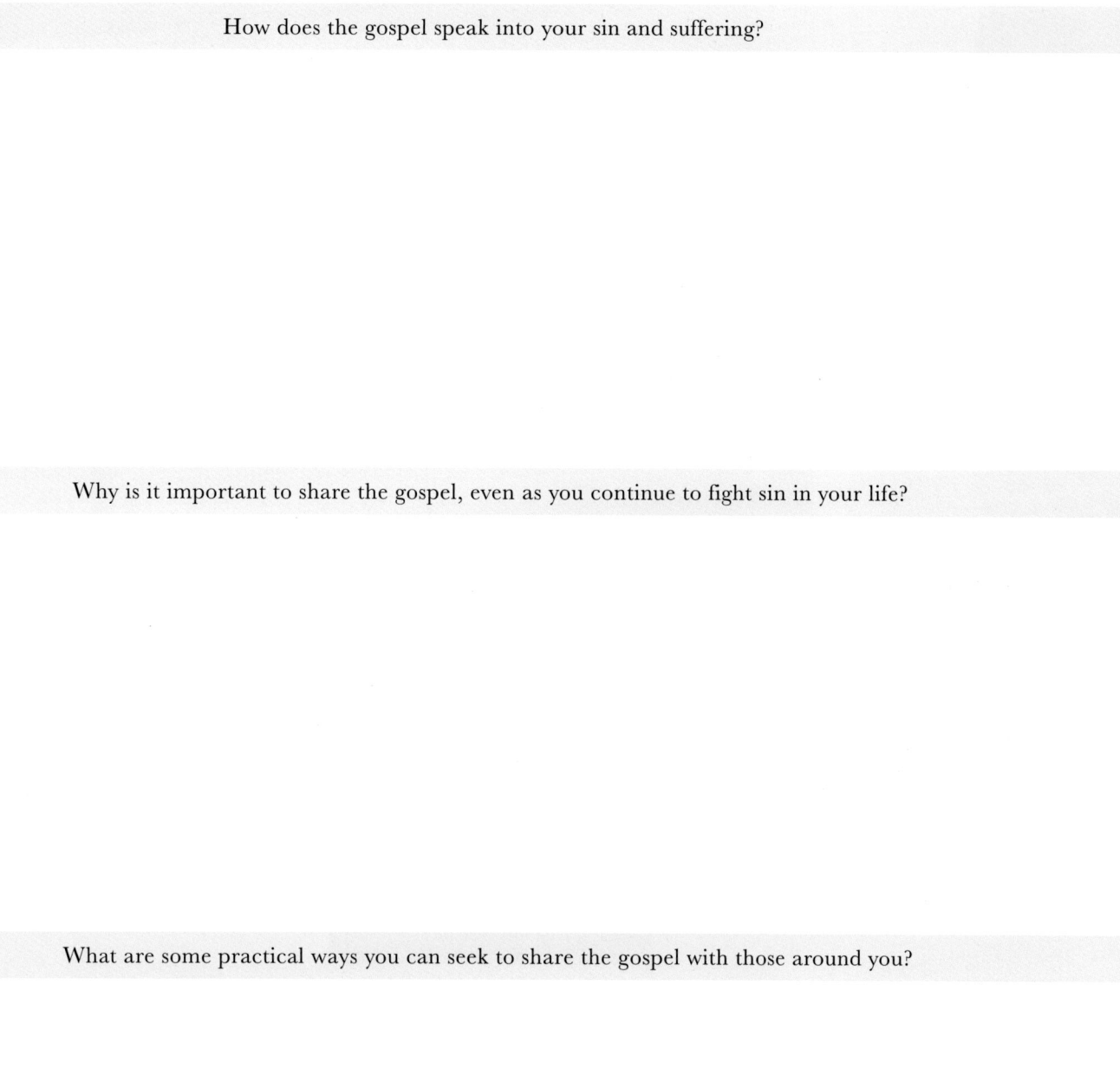

How does the gospel speak into your sin and suffering?

Why is it important to share the gospel, even as you continue to fight sin in your life?

What are some practical ways you can seek to share the gospel with those around you?

WEEK 3 / DAY 5

Jesus Christ is our only hope in deliverance from evil.

Victory in Jesus

READ 1 CORINTHIANS 15:50-58

The temptation in studying the armor of God is to attempt to ensure certain disciplinary actions must take place in order to measure up as Christians. We may assume we can muster up our own strength and sufficiency against sin and temptation. But when we look back to Old Testament passages of God wearing the armor for Himself, we are reminded that it is truly God's armor given to us. God is the divine warrior. His armor does not exist apart from Him, and the armor only proves to be sufficient through Him. The armor is not our own, yet He has given it to His people as active weaponry and protection in this life.

From beginning to end, the Bible tells the story of God's plan to fully and finally deliver His people from evil. In Genesis, we see the first glimpse of God's plan to crush Satan. We continue through the Old Testament and see the promise of a seed through the line of Abraham (Genesis 26:3-5, Galatians 3:16) and the prophecy of a child in Isaiah (Isaiah 7:14). We see leaders like Moses (Deuteronomy 18:17-18) and kings like David (2 Samuel 7:12-13), pointing us toward a better King and leader. Regardless of the sinful and evil circumstances that sought to undo this promise, God protected it. And in the gospels, this promise was born (Luke 2). This promise is fulfilled in Jesus Christ, the Savior of the world, our rescuer and deliverer. He lived among us, fully man and fully God, knowing that the cross was set before Him. His death purchased redemption for God's people, and His resurrection defeated death once and for all.

Jesus Christ is our only hope in deliverance from evil. We are incapable in and of ourselves. When we take on the righteousness of Christ, we put to death the desires of the flesh. In Christ, we share in His victory and are equipped to face the remaining evils of this world. Yet, we are not simply thrown into the arena and instructed to fight in our own strength. We are equipped with God's armor to wage war and are strengthened by the Holy Spirit so that we might stand against Satan's schemes. We fasten the belt of truth around our waists as we trust in the truth of who God is to hold us secure, while the breastplate of righteousness covers us with the righteousness of Christ. We strap on sandals fitted with the gospel of peace as we prepare to take the gospel to a weary and waiting world. Our faith serves as our shield, guarding us against fear as we press onward, and the helmet of salvation gives hope beyond the present battles we face. Finally, the sword of the Spirit, which is the Word of God, brings us wisdom and discernment in every circumstance, trial, and temptation we face.

As we strive to dress in the armor of God and walk in obedience, we take refuge in the hope and the promise that we *will* be delivered from evil. Because God is transcendent, or outside of this sphere of time, and has already defeated sin, we live in waiting for our promised deliverance to be fully realized in eternity with Him. The armor of God encourages us to face each day and the battles they bring. It encourages us to pray with an urgency that Jesus would come soon, for when He comes, all will be made right in the world. Stumbling blocks or enticement toward sin will crumble. Christ will defeat evil once and for all. As we pray for these things, our purchased hope is that victory awaits us too. Jesus Christ triumphs over evil through His death and resurrection, and His victory is credited to all who put their hope and faith in Him. He stood firm against every temptation and trial in His life, even to the point of death. We are weak, fearful, unprepared, and too easily lured into sin by our deceitful desires—yet we will stand with Him. The gospel is good news that speaks of ordinary sinners rescued by an extraordinary God in such a way that even the combined forces of hell could never steal us from Him. Satan is strong, but the stronger One has bound and defeated him. May we put on the armor of God and rest in the hope that Jesus Christ has already won the war.

> "
> The gospel is good news that speaks of ordinary sinners rescued by *an extraordinary God.*

daily questions

What new insights did you learn from this study on the armor of God?

How do you feel encouraged and equipped to fight sin in your life with the armor of God?

In what ways will you daily seek to dress in God's armor while ultimately remembering your secured hope in final victory with Jesus?

> *May we put on the armor of God and rest in the hope that Jesus Christ has already won the war.*

Scripture Memory

Ephesians 6:18-20

Pray at all times in the Spirit with every prayer and request, and stay alert with all perseverance and intercession for all the saints.

Pray also for me, that the message may be given to me when I open my mouth to make known with boldness the mystery of the gospel.

For this I am an ambassador in chains. Pray that I might be bold enough to speak about it as I should.

Weekly Reflection

EPHESIANS 6:18-20; 1 CORINTHIANS 15:50-58

Paraphrase the passage from this week.

What did you observe from this week's text about God and His character?

What do this week's passage reveal about the condition of mankind and yourself?

How does this passage point to the gospel?

How should you respond to this passage? What specific action steps can you take this week to apply this passage?

Write a prayer in response to your study of God's Word. Adore God for who He is, confess sins that He revealed in your own life, ask Him to empower you to walk in obedience, and pray for anyone who comes to mind as you study.

Weekly Reflection / 85

The Full Armor of God

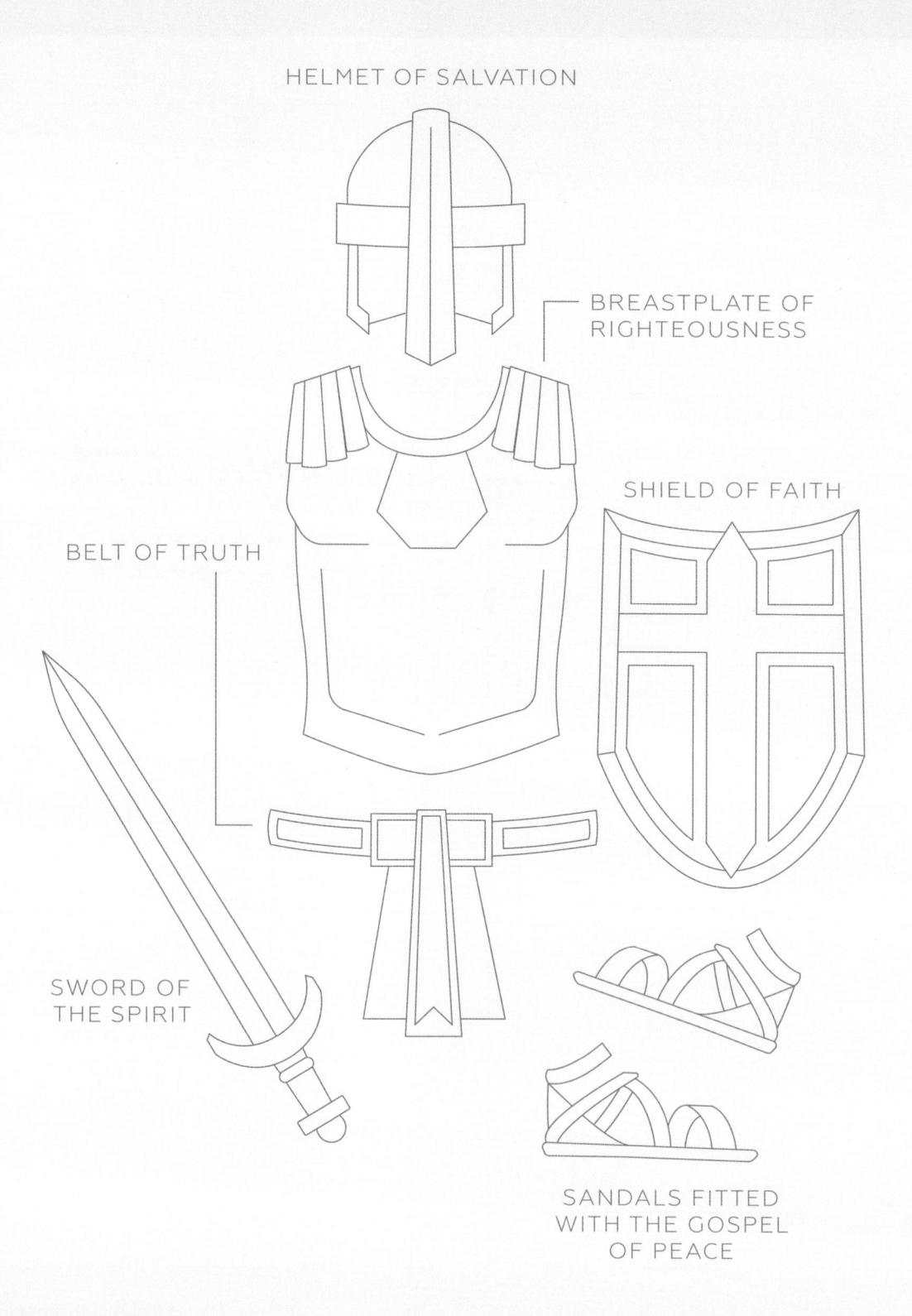

HELMET OF SALVATION

BREASTPLATE OF RIGHTEOUSNESS

SHIELD OF FAITH

BELT OF TRUTH

SWORD OF THE SPIRIT

SANDALS FITTED WITH THE GOSPEL OF PEACE

Summarize the purpose of each specific piece of armor.

Belt of Truth

Breastplate of Righteousness

Sandals fitted with the gospel of peace

Shield of Faith

Helmet of Salvation

Sword of the Spirit

Old Testament References

FOR EACH PIECE OF ARMOR

The Belt of Truth

ISAIAH 11:5   Righteousness will be a belt around his hips;
faithfulness will be a belt around his waist.

*Faithfulness in this passage can also be translated to mean truthfulness.

Breastplate of Righteousness

ISAIAH 59:16-17   He saw that there was no man—
he was amazed that there was no one interceding;
so his own arm brought salvation,
and his own righteousness supported him.
He put on **righteousness as body armor**,
and a helmet of salvation on his head;
he put on garments of vengeance for clothing,
and he wrapped himself in zeal as in a cloak.

Sandals Fitted with the Gospel of Peace

ISAIAH 52:7   How beautiful on the mountains
are the **feet** of the herald,
who proclaims **peace**,
who brings **news of good things**,
who proclaims salvation,
who says to Zion, "Your God reigns!"

Shield of Faith

PSALM 3:3   But you, Lord, are a **shield** around me,
my glory, and the one who lifts up my head.

Helmet of Salvation

ISAIAH 59:16-17   He saw that there was no man—
he was amazed that there was no one interceding;
so his own arm brought salvation,
and his own righteousness supported him.
He put on righteousness as body armor,
and a **helmet of salvation** on his head;
he put on garments of vengeance for clothing,
and he wrapped himself in zeal as in a cloak.

Sword of the Spirit

ISAIAH 49:2   He made my words like **a sharp sword**;
he hid me in the shadow of his hand.
He made me like a sharpened arrow;
he hid me in his quiver.

What is the Gospel?

THANK YOU FOR READING AND ENJOYING THIS STUDY WITH US! WE ARE ABUNDANTLY GRATEFUL FOR THE WORD OF GOD, THE INSTRUCTION WE GLEAN FROM IT, AND THE EVER-GROWING UNDERSTANDING IT PROVIDES FOR US OF GOD'S CHARACTER. WE ARE ALSO THANKFUL THAT SCRIPTURE CONTINUALLY POINTS TO ONE THING IN INNUMERABLE WAYS: THE GOSPEL.

We remember our brokenness when we read about the fall of Adam and Eve in the garden of Eden (Genesis 3), where sin entered into a perfect world and maimed it. We remember the necessity that something innocent must die to pay for our sin when we read about the atoning sacrifices in the Old Testament. We read that we have all sinned and fallen short of the glory of God (Romans 3:23) and that the penalty for our brokenness, the wages of our sin, is death (Romans 6:23). We all need grace and mercy, but most importantly, we all need a Savior.

We consider the goodness of God when we realize that He did not plan to leave us in this dire state. We see His promise to buy us back from the clutches of sin and death in Genesis 3:15. And we see that promise accomplished with Jesus Christ on the cross. Jesus Christ knew no sin yet became sin so that we might become righteous through His sacrifice (2 Corinthians 5:21). Jesus was tempted in every way that we are and lived sinlessly. He was reviled yet still yielded Himself for our sake, that we may have life abundant in Him. Jesus lived the perfect life that we could not live and died the death that we deserved.

The gospel is profound yet simple. There are many mysteries in it that we will never understand this side of heaven, but there is still overwhelming weight to its implications in this life. The gospel tells of our sinfulness and God's goodness and a gracious gift that compels a response. We are saved by grace through faith, which means that we rest with faith in the grace that Jesus Christ displayed on the cross (Ephesians 2:8-9). We cannot save ourselves from our brokenness or do any amount of good works to merit God's favor. Still, we can have faith that what Jesus accomplished in His death, burial, and resurrection was more than enough for our salvation and our eternal delight. When we accept God, we are commanded to die to ourselves and our sinful desires and live a life worthy of the calling we have received (Ephesians 4:1). The gospel compels us to be sanctified, and in so doing, we are conformed to the likeness of Christ Himself. This is hope. This is redemption. This is the gospel.

SCRIPTURES TO REFERENCE:

GENESIS 3:15	*I will put hostility between you and the woman, and between your offspring and her offspring. He will strike your head, and you will strike his heel.*
ROMANS 3:23	*For all have sinned and fall short of the glory of God.*
ROMANS 6:23	*For the wages of sin is death, but the gift of God is eternal life in Christ Jesus our Lord.*
2 CORINTHIANS 5:21	*He made the one who did not know sin to be sin for us, so that in him we might become the righteousness of God.*
EPHESIANS 2:8-9	*For you are saved by grace through faith, and this is not from yourselves; it is God's gift — not from works, so that no one can boast.*
EPHESIANS 4:1-3	*Therefore I, the prisoner in the Lord, urge you to walk worthy of the calling you have received, with all humility and gentleness, with patience, bearing with one another in love, making every effort to keep the unity of the Spirit through the bond of peace.*

*Thank you for studying
God's Word with us!*

CONNECT WITH US
@thedailygraceco
@dailygracepodcast
@kristinschmucker

CONTACT US
info@thedailygraceco.com

SHARE
#thedailygraceco
#lampandlight

VISIT US ONLINE
www.thedailygraceco.com

MORE DAILY GRACE
The Daily Grace App
Daily Grace Podcast